HORRIBLE SCIENCE

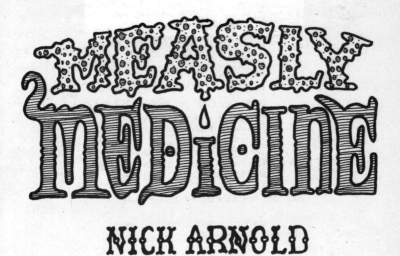

MEASLY MEDICINE

NICK ARNOLD

Illustrated by
Tony De Saulles

■SCHOLA

Scholastic Children's Books,
Euston House, 24 Eversholt Street,
London NW1 1DB, UK

A division of Scholastic Ltd
London ~ New York ~ Toronto ~ Sydney ~ Auckland
Mexico City ~ New Delhi ~ Hong Kong

First published in the UK by Scholastic Ltd, 2006

Text copyright © Nick Arnold, 2006
Illustrations copyright © Tony De Saulles, 2006

10 digit ISBN 0 439 95581 5
13 digit ISBN 978 0439 95581 2

Printed and bound by Nørhaven Paperback A/S, Denmark

2 4 6 8 10 9 7 5 3 1

Contents

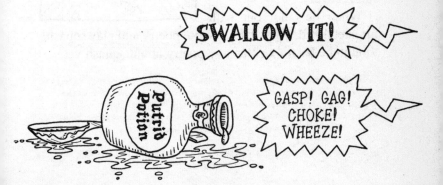

SWALLOW IT!

Putrid Potion

GASP! GAG!
CHOKE!
WHEEZE!

Nick Arnold has been writing stories and books since he was a youngster, but never dreamt he'd find fame writing about measly medicine. His research involved sitting in the potty patient chair and he enjoyed every minute of it.

When he's not delving into Horrible Science, he spends his spare time eating pizza, riding his bike and thinking up corny jokes (though not all at the same time).

Tony De Saulles picked up his crayons when he was still in nappies and has been doodling ever since. He takes Horrible Science very seriously and even agreed to sample tortoise brains. Fortunately, he has made a full recovery.

When he's not out with his sketchpad, Tony likes to write poetry and play squash, though he hasn't written any poetry about squash yet.

INTRODUCTION

If there's one thing worse than being ill – it's getting cured. I mean, who actually enjoys seeing the doctor and taking vile medicine? It can really leave a nasty taste in your mouth!

I HATE MEDICINE!

IT'S ENOUGH TO MAKE YOU SICK!

But as this book shows, there's more to medicine than pills, ills and dreary doctors. Just listen to Dr Grimgrave, our very own miserable medical expert…

MEDICINE IS THE SCIENCE OF HEALTH AND ANY TREATMENT FOR ILL-HEALTH…

AND IT'S GOOD FOR YOU – SO STOP COMPLAINING!

Dr Grimgrave's got a point. Medicine is about healing and we all need it because we all get ill. It can even save your life. So read on to find out where medicine came from and where it's going. You'll discover that medicine in the past was even more measly. There were…

• Rotten remedies

• Odious operations

• Murderous medical mistakes

You'll end up wickedly well informed about them all and who knows? You might even give your doctors a taste of their own medicine…

Well, one thing's for sure – being ill won't seem quite so bad!

HORRIBLE HEALTHCARE

We're watching a TV hospital drama…

Before we drop in on Dr Grimgrave there are a few things you need to know…

Everything you need to know about Dr Grimgrave but were afraid to ask

NAME: Dr H Grimgrave (He won't tell us his first name – I bet it's embarrassing.)

AGE: Wasn't that him on the front cover? Surely he's not that old!

JOB: Local doctor, also known as a physician, general practitioner or GP. Dr G provides primary care. He treats sick people, and no, "treats" doesn't means he takes patients to the zoo and buys them ice creams. As if! It means he gives them medical treatment. If necessary he sends them to hospital (secondary care).

LIKES: An empty surgery.

DISLIKES: "Idiot" patients who aren't really ill.

DON'T MENTION: Baldness (Dr G is rather sensitive). Oh, and don't laugh whilst you're reading this book. Dr G is extremely serious even when he tells dreadful doctor jokes. OK, you can read on now…

A day at the doctor's

Dr Grimgrave has agreed to let us watch him treating one of our sick readers. There are lots more sick people in his waiting room, and it's a great place to find out what can go wrong with the poor battered body…

8

1 Disease

There are hundreds of different diseases. Some can be inherited from your parents; but many are caused by germs – microbes such as bacteria and viruses. There are several ways in which germs can sneak into your body…

• By being breathed in
• By being eaten or drunk
• Through a cut or wound

And they multiply – poisoning and killing the tiny cells that make up your body. When this happens it's called an "infection".

2 Unhealthy lifestyle

Some diseases are linked to an unhealthy lifestyle. For example, doctors blame heart attacks on eating too many fatty foods and lack of exercise. Smoking is linked to heart attacks and diseases such as cancer.

3 Injury

The body can get injured through accidents or violence. It can suffer…

- Broken bones
- Cuts to the skin
- Burns and scalds
- Bashes and bruises
- Stab or bullet wounds

4 Childbirth

Getting pregnant and giving birth can cause great changes to a woman's body. In the past giving birth was dangerous and many women died (see page 116).

5 Old age

Even if you survive disease, injury and childbirth, old age catches up on everyone (although your ancient teachers will probably NOT admit this). The weakening of the body in old age causes problems such as failing eyesight, loss of hearing and painful joints.

Dr Grimgrave says…

ILL HEALTH AND DISEASE GET TO US ALL IN THE END.

TELL ME ABOUT IT!

At last it's our turn to see Dr Grimgrave. We knock politely on his door and enter his consulting room. He greets us with a question…

The effects of diseases are called "symptoms" and doctors are trained to spot them…

Bet you never knew!
17th-century doctor Thomas Sydenham (1624–1689) described the symptoms of gout – a painful disease of the toe joints. This is more or less what he said…

The victim goes to bed and sleeps in good health. About 2 o'clock he is awakened by a severe pain in the big toe … it cannot bear the weight of the bedclothes nor the movement of a person walking in the room. The night is passed in torture…

Thomas Sydenham suffered from gout. He was writing about himself.

The doctor will want to find out if the disease is something you've inherited or is linked to your unhealthy lifestyle…

BLOCKED NOSES RUN IN OUR FAMILY

HOW UNHYGIENIC!

In fact, the doctor won't always believe you. Many people claim to eat healthier food or take more exercise than they really do. Doctors often make notes about what you tell them. This is because they are too busy to remember anything anyone tells them. Notes used to be handwritten but nowadays most doctors use computers…

Bet you never knew!
Doctors' handwriting is said to be almost impossible to read. In 2000 a hospital in Atlanta City, USA gave doctors handwriting classes. Is anyone brave enough to suggest a handwriting class for Dr Grimgrave?

After asking you about your symptoms, the doctor will often examine your body. He or she will be looking for obvious symptoms such as redness (inflammation), spots, rashes, lumps, swellings or a furry tongue. The doctor might also take swabs or samples to be tested in the lab for disease-causing microbes. General practitioners often use equipment to help them examine the patient. Here's a very rare glimpse inside Dr Grimgrave's medical bag.

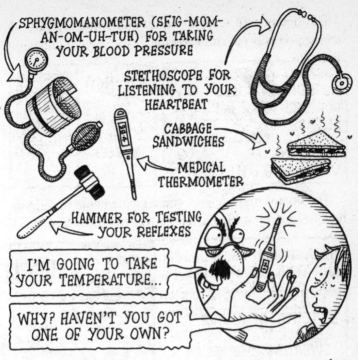

At last the doctor has enough information to say what the patient is suffering from. This is called diagnosis. Let's watch Dr G in action…

Dr Grimgrave in … Cold comfort

The doctor will tell you how the disease is likely to develop. This is called prognosis.

The doctor may suggest you take medicine or tell you how to treat your illness. This is called a prescription.

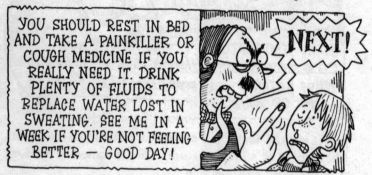

In fact, 80–90 per cent of all diseases are healed by the body's own anti-germ defences based on white blood cells. Your superb cells work together like an army to wipe out the gruesome germs. Some act as sentries that spot the germs, others make anti-germ substances called antibodies that can kill or glue the germs together. Other white blood cells gobble up the gummed-together germs. And the bottom line is that many patients don't need to see a doctor in order to get better!

So that's what happens when you see the doctor. But now an incredibly important point ... ahem!

An incredibly important point

Everything you've seen in this chapter was invented by someone. Let's find out who these incredible inventors were…

Blood transfusion

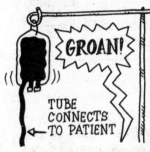

A transfusion is when a patient is given blood to replace blood they've lost through injury. It was made possible by Austrian scientist Karl Landsteiner (1868–1943) who found we each have one of four blood groups and only certain types will mix. He was no clot.

ECG machine (brainy boffins call it an electrocardiograph).

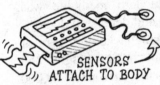

Monitors tiny electrical pulses made by the heart. It was invented by Dutch scientist Willem Einthoven (1860–1927) in 1903.

Defibrillator

A machine for shocking failing hearts to make them beat. It was first used to save a life by US surgeon Claude Beck in 1947.

Diagnosis, Prognosis and Prescription

Invented way back in around 400 BC by the glorious Greek physician Hippocrates (see page 25).

15

Medical thermometer

ALLBUTT'S DESIGN

MODERN DIGITAL VERSION

Invented by Thomas Clifford Allbutt (1836–1925) in 1867. Before then thermometers were 30 cm long and took 20 minutes to work.

Sphygmomanometer

First invented by Julius Hérisson in 1835 but improved a lot since then.

Stethoscope

Invented by French doctor René Laënnec (1781–1826) in 1816.

Got the idea? Everything in modern medicine was discovered by suffering scientists and dedicated doctors. The rest of this book tells the whole sickening story of medicine complete with brilliant breakthroughs and measly mistakes. Our story begins in a cave about 20,000 years ago…

COUGH, SPLUTTER, I FEEL DREADFUL!

DON'T WORRY – I'VE JUST INVENTED MEDICINE!

AWESOME ANCIENT DOCTORS

Stone Age people had some surprisingly effective treatments… Mind you, one of them was as welcome as a hole in the head!

I KNOW – I TRIED IT!

Five surprisingly effective Stone Age treatments

1 Setting bones (using a splint to hold the broken ends of a bone together so that it can heal). Splints are still used today.

2 Amputation (that's posh medical-speak for cutting off diseased arms, legs, fingers, toes, etc). Modern surgeons still do this in an emergency.

3 Healing herbs. The herb catnip grew near Stone Age houses and it might have been grown as a remedy for upset Stone-Age stomachs. Mind you, catnip drives cats wild, so it might have been for playful prehistoric pets too.

CATNIP

CAT-NIPPERS

4 Stitching wounds. Stone Age people probably knew how to sew up wounds using bone needles. Modern surgeons still stitch up wounds, although they don't use bone needles.

5 Trepanning. And if you think that's hitting a tree with metal pan, you really do need your head examined! It means scraping a hole in someone's skull with a sharp piece of flint or drilling a hole with a pointed stick until their brain was revealed. Oh well, it helps to keep a cool head...

Those Stone Age surgeons must have been bold even if they left their patients bald and holed.

GRRR – BALDNESS IS NO LAUGHING MATTER!

Dr Grimgrave

No one is sure why Stone Age people did trepanning but it was amazingly widespread. Skulls with holes in them have been found all over the world.

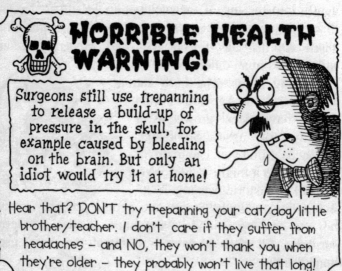

☠ HORRIBLE HEALTH WARNING!

Surgeons still use trepanning to release a build-up of pressure in the skull, for example caused by bleeding on the brain. But only an idiot would try it at home!

Hear that? DON'T try trepanning your cat/dog/little brother/teacher. I don't care if they suffer from headaches – and NO, they won't thank you when they're older – they probably won't live that long!

Why not practise your skills on an innocent melon instead?

Dare you discover ... trepanning a melon

What you need:
A melon. Watermelons are good because they're green on the outside and red and mushy on the inside – just like a sickly human patient!
A sharp pencil
A table knife (a blunt one)
A felt pen and a touch of artistic flair
Tweezers

What you do:
1 Draw a face on your melon. If the face happens to look like your teacher you're on your own, OK?
2 Press the point of your pencil gently into the top of the melon. Place the pencil between your hands and rub them backwards and forwards to make the pencil "drill" through the melon's skin.
3 Take care not to drill into the melon's brain, er, flesh. You don't want to KILL your patient now, do you?
4 When you've drilled one hole, drill another six or seven about 2 cm apart so they form a circle.
5 Use your knife to cut between the holes. Once again take care not to damage the flesh. Your melon will be bleeding juice, but you're a doctor so a bit of gore won't put you off, will it?

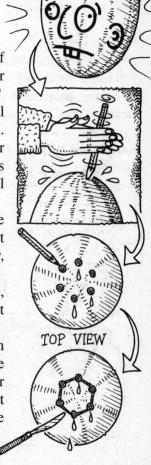

TOP VIEW

6 Use your tweezers to lift off the circle of melon and expose the brain flesh underneath.

7 Hopefully your melon will be feeling a lot better, but if it doesn't survive the op you can always eat it with your favourite topping. And you can't do that with a human patient!

Sickly cities

About 9,000 years ago people began to settle in cities and you might think that was a good thing. I mean, there are lots more shops and pizza restaurants. But cities were sickly. There were more neighbours to catch diseases from, and scientists who study ancient mummies have found they suffered from diseases that people still get today. Dr Grimgrave is examining a measly mummy...

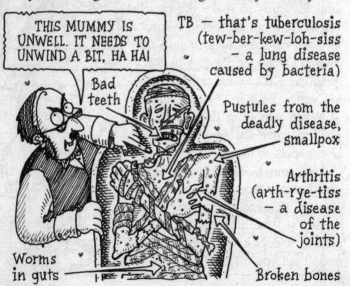

THIS MUMMY IS UNWELL. IT NEEDS TO UNWIND A BIT, HA HA!

Bad teeth

TB — that's tuberculosis (tew-ber-kew-loh-siss — a lung disease caused by bacteria)

Pustules from the deadly disease, smallpox

Arthritis (arth-rye-tiss — a disease of the joints)

Worms in guts

Broken bones

The Egyptians tried thousands of treatments. So which of these would you try on your mummy?

Horrible Healthcare presents...

ANCIENT EGYPTIAN CURES YOU'LL BE DYING TO TRY!

TOOTHACHE? – DON'T SUFFER IN SILENCE!

Try new **RO–DENTURE!**

Split open a mouse and lay its warm body along your gums. You're sure to squeak through – even if the mouse doesn't!

SSSLUB!

UNDER THE WEATHER? Try new

GARLIC GARGLE

– now with EXTRA garlic! It's guaranteed to tackle terrible toothache. And it's sure to get rid of sore throats AND unwanted visitors! Try it on your dog and his bark will be worse than his bite!

UGH!

Is this "toe" good to be true? Accidents will happen, but if you find yourself short of a few toes, don't despair! Egyptian doctors have invented...

THE WOODY-TIDDLER WOODEN BIG TOE

Lovely choice of woods and colours!

"My toenails look great with wood varnish and they never need cutting!" Satisfied patient.

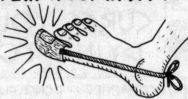

Tired of weeping wounds? Cure your cuts with new

MILKY PLOPS!

POOEY PONG!

Milky Plops contain the finest high-quality poo and full-cream milk. You plop them on your wounds and they'll heal in a flush, er, flash.

It's a sight for sore eyes! If your eyes have cloudy areas (cataracts), why not try

BRAINY-BALM?

It's made from genuine chopped-up tortoise brains mixed with honey.

SMEAR IT ON YOUR EYEBALLS MORNING AND NIGHT TO PUT YOUR SIGHT RIGHT.

Well, I bet the tortoise brains helped your memory – you might have got "turtle recall"!

But to be fair, Egyptian docs were only doing their best. And some of their medicines included germ-killing substances such as honey and the plant myrrh.

Bet you never knew!
One Egyptian doctor Imhotep (lived around 2900 BC) became a god! Incredible Immy could diagnose over 200 diseases and perform surgery. And that's not all – he became prime minister to King Zoser and designed the famous Step Pyramid. I bet that was a step up in the world! Immy was made a god in 525 BC and he would have felt divine if he hadn't been dead for more than 2,000 years.

BETTER LATE THAN NEVER!

The glorious Greeks

Like their near neighbours the Egyptians, the ancient Greeks had a doctor god. His name was Asclepius and some experts think he was once a real person. If you were poorly you went to the god's temple to ask for help. And stayed for a sickly sleepover party…

 GROAN!

Poorly?

MOAN!

Come and stay at our luxury temple of Asclepius!

INSTRUCTIONS

1. Sacrifice a ram (bring your own) to the gods.

 EEK!

2. Take a bath – it's the best route to a clean bill of health!

AND YOU CAN WASH OFF THE RAM'S BLOOD!

 WELL, HELLLLO!

3. Go to sleep. This cure works like a dream! In the night the god visits with his daughters Panacea and Hygeia.

4. You wake up cured ... er, maybe. Well, if you don't you can always enjoy an extended stay, with lots of massage and a nice healthy diet.

BLAST! BRING ME ANOTHER RAM!

∘ ∘ ∘ ∘ ✳ THE SMALL PRINT ✳ ∘ ∘ ∘ ∘

1. Our temple is crawling with snakes – but don't worry they're symbols of healing! **2.** If you die don't tell anyone – it's bad for business. In fact we'll hide your body in the woods! **3.** It doesn't cost anything to sleep over but you have to give us a gold model of your poorly body bit. This could cost you an (golden) arm or a leg.

Notice anything? The ancient Greeks reckoned healing was about gods rather than science. Like most ancient people, they didn't imagine ill health could have natural causes.

Bet you never knew!
The ancient Assyrians (who lived in present-day Iraq) believed that disease was caused by up to 900 spirits. Some lived in your food and drink. Adults still feel ill after drinking spirits, but it's not quite the same thing.

One of the first people to suggest that disease had natural causes was a top doc named Hippocrates (460–377 BC). As you can see, he lived to a ripe old age. Well, you didn't expect him to live to an under-ripe young age, did you?

Hippo was a teacher. He taught under a plane tree on the Greek island of Cos, and I bet he made everything plane to his students. It's said he wrote over 60 books but other people may have written some of them. Anyway here's a selection of Hippo's sayings to share with your ancient Greek teacher…

Old people endure hunger best, next the middle-aged, youths and worst of all children.

It's not true — I'm starving.

Do not judge poo by its quantity but by its quality.

I'm not so hungry now...

The old are ill less than the young but carry their illnesses to the grave.

YOU'VE GONE TOO FAR!

Sudden death is commoner in the fat than the thin...

GRRRR — I'LL GIVE YOU SUDDEN DEATH!

Hippo had a huge impact on later doctors and I don't mean he jumped on top of them...

Measly medicine fact file

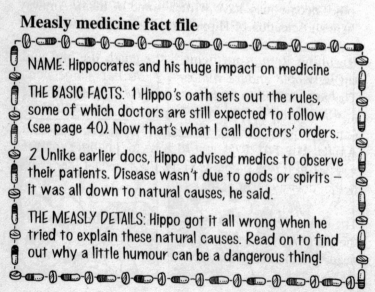

NAME: Hippocrates and his huge impact on medicine

THE BASIC FACTS: 1 Hippo's oath sets out the rules, some of which doctors are still expected to follow (see page 40). Now that's what I call doctors' orders.

2 Unlike earlier docs, Hippo advised medics to observe their patients. Disease wasn't due to gods or spirits — it was all down to natural causes, he said.

THE MEASLY DETAILS: Hippo got it all wrong when he tried to explain these natural causes. Read on to find out why a little humour can be a dangerous thing!

Horrible humours

Hippocrates reckoned that everything was made of earth, air, fire and water, and that included the human body. According to Hippo people were made of earthy, airy, fiery or watery substances called humours. They are black bile, yellow bile, blood and phlegm. (By the way, phlegm is not only the gloopy stuff you cough up – it's also mucus or snot.) Hippo thought that people got ill because their humours were out of balance … but he was wrong.

The trouble really began when the Romans used Hippo's ideas in ways that actually *harmed* patients…

Revolting Roman medicine – the good, the bad and the ugly

The good… Roman surgeons were good, especially their army surgeons who got lots of practice treating wounds (can you guess why?). One superb surgeon, Aetius of Amida (AD 502–575) knew how to tie arteries (the vessels that carry blood from the heart) over 1,000 years before doctors relearnt the skill.

The bad… The Romans tried some terrible treatments. If they suffered from fainting fits they drank the blood of dead gladiators. Slaves were given cabbage as a treatment. The cabbage cure was invented by politician Cato the Censor (234–149 BC) who claimed that cabbage cured all known diseases in cattle and slaves – but especially cattle because they were worth more. He wrote about his discovery in a book. Here's a verse version…

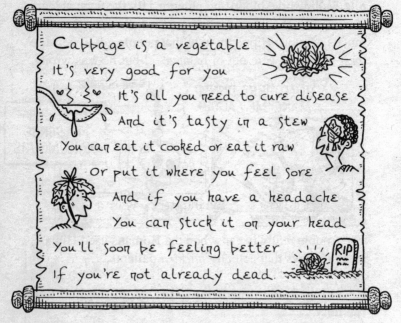

Cabbage is a vegetable
It's very good for you
It's all you need to cure disease
And it's tasty in a stew
You can eat it cooked or eat it raw
Or put it where you feel sore
And if you have a headache
You can stick it on your head
You'll soon be feeling better
If you're not already dead.

Cruel Cato advised slave owners to "get rid" of slaves who weren't cured by cabbage. And if the slaves survived, I bet they ended up with a bad bottom-burp problem.

The ugly… The most important doctor in Rome was a Greek with a really ugly temper and even uglier ideas. Galen (AD 130–201) was a brilliantly brainy bigheaded bossy bully. So of course, we just *had* to meet him…

Fortunately there's a TV show that digs up dead celebs for that final farewell interview…

With us tonight is Galen. So what's it like to be dead?

I'm a bored stiff.

You started your career at the gladiator school where you studied wounds.

Yes I had a stab at it...

You were doctor to several Roman emperors.

By Jupiter, I was a genius!

Your books were read for 1,500 years. It's a pity they were wrong!

You what?!

You believed in humours, you said that blood is made in the liver and gets mixed with an invisible life-giving gas in the lungs and gets used up in the body. You tried to heal wounds with pigeons' blood — ALL WRONG!*

*You'll find more of Galen's measly mistakes on page 80.

CONTINUED

It was humours that did the damage. Hippocrates didn't bleed patients too often and to be fair nor did Galen, but reckless writers such as Cornelius Celsus (1st century AD) reckoned that if too much blood caused disease, then bleeding made you better. And you could get rid of other humours by raising painful blisters or making yourself sick, or making yourself poo…

European doctors used these terrible treatments for hundreds of years. So let's leave them to it and check out what was going on in the rest of the world.

THE MEASLY MEDICAL WORLD TOUR

All over the world measly medics invented their own ways to heal their even more measly patients… So where would you prefer to be sick?

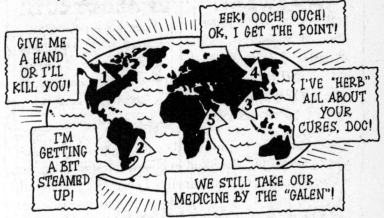

1 North America Chants and sweat lodges to purify the body. Medicines used include herbs, buffalo stomach stones and an enemy's dried fingers – well, that's a handy remedy.

2 South America Traditional Mayan and Aztec medicine based on herbs and steam baths.

3 India The great Indian doctor Charaka writes a book on medicine around 1000 BC. Indian docs are trained in herbal remedies and seriously sensational surgery.

4 China Traditional Chinese medicine starts with Emperor Huang-di around 2600 BC. Lots of herbal remedies and acupuncture (see page 34).

5 Middle East Arabs conquer the area in 7th century AD and preserve books by Galen and Hippocrates. OK, they preserved their measly mistakes too, but nobody's perfect. Most towns have hospitals, and universities teach medicine.

GET BETTER THE AZTEC WAY!

FEVER CURE? NO SWEAT!

If you've got a fever why not enjoy a relaxing steam bath? It'll get you better and it's no sweat! Well, there'll be quite a lot of sweat actually...

DON'T GET CUT UP ABOUT CUTS!

Pour some powdered obsidian glass into them. It might seem a sharp remedy, but we think it speeds up healing!

OOPS, SORRY, MADAM!

THIS GLASS IS A "PANE"!

TRY NEW RUBBERLUG!

If earache is spoiling your life why not pour liquid rubber into your ear holes? It's something to sound off about!

EH?

DON'T GET SNIFFY ABOUT COLDS!

Simply collect dew from the fields and plop a drop in each nostril. You'll soon feel fresh as a daisy!

HOW "DEW" FEEL?

WARNING TO ANYONE PLANNING TO BE ILL IN AZTEC TIMES! BEWARE – you might end up being sacrificed to the gods by beastly priests who will cut out your heart and eat bits of your body. At least you won't get any of that nasty sickness (anyone who eats you might get it but that's their problem!).

The amazing East

Doctors in ancient China and India developed their own styles of healing. They never actually met, so we thought it was good idea to bring them together…

Your body turns your food into vital energy.

We think the body's life force is called qui.

Air, bile and phlegm go around the body. You need them for health but too much makes you ill. And demons make you ill too.

No it's the body's life force that gets out of balance. We diagnose disease by feeling your pulse.

We know hundreds of herbal remedies.

So do we. Emperor Shen Nong described 365 medical herbs that he tested on himself — including the poisonous ones.

INDIAN DOCTOR

CHINESE DOCTOR

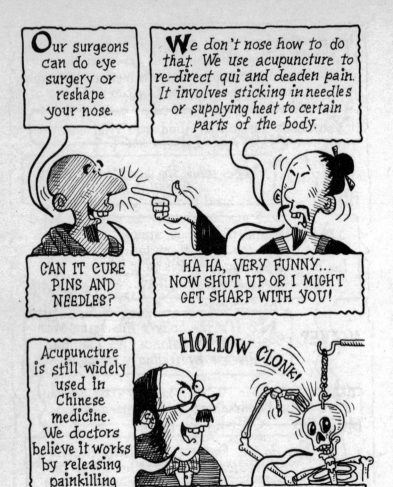

Acupuncture was invented before 1000 BC. No one knows who hit on the idea but I guess they had sharp wits. Anyway, here's an ancient Chinese doc we do know about. And his life was so dramatic I've turned it into a traditional Chinese opera.

THE STORY OF HUA TUO (AD 110–207)

Music: All the words are sung loudly to the sound of Chinese drums and cymbals, etc. (You can perform it at 4 am but don't blame me if you suffer a similar fate to Hua tuo.)

CURTAIN UP ~ ACT 1

Scene: A village.

ENTER HUA TUO AS A YOUNG MAN.

HUA: Life is hard and death is easy. My poor mum depends on me since dad died and my brother was taken away to work for the Emperor.

MOTHER: Son, I'm poorly – can you help me?

HUA: Mother I'll try, I know a little medicine...

MOTHER: Erk! (DIES)

HUA: But not enough it seems... I shall become a doctor and save lives in the future.

NARRATOR: Hua was as good as his word. He walked across China to train with a famous doctor. Within six years Hua was a famous healer, too. His future looked healthy – or did it?

(END OF ACT 1)

ACT 2

Scene: A palace.

ENTER THE GOVERNOR, HIS SON AND SERVANTS.

GOVERNOR: Let's see what Hua tuo suggests to make me better...

(READS → FROM PIECE OF PAPER) "THE GOVERNOR IS A STUPID TWIT WITH A BIG NOSE" – Agggh! I'll kill that cheeky doctor! Gurgle – now I'm sicking up blood!

SON: (FALLS TO KNEES) Don't kill him, Dad. Hua tuo said he had to make you cross in order to cure you. It was part of his plan.

GOVERNOR: (WIPING MOUTH WITH SLEEVE) Odd that – I feel better already. Hua tuo is a genius!

NARRATOR: Hua tuo's fame spread even more. It's said he was the first doctor to cut out a patient's appendix. So he really was a cut above the rest!

(END OF ACT 2)

ACT 3

Scene: Another palace.

ENTER PRINCE CAO CAO, GUARDS AND HUA TUO.

PRINCE: Hua tuo, I insist you become my personal doctor. Only you can heal my horrible hammering headaches.

HUA TUO: Great prince, I want to be free to heal everyone – not just you. I think I'll go home. (EXIT HUA TUO)

PRINCE: He'll regret it! If he won't be my doctor he won't be anyone's. Guards – KILL THAT DOCTOR!

GUARDS: Yes, Your Majesty! (EXIT GUARDS)

Off stage: SOUND OF MUFFLED SCREAM AND BODY BEING DRAGGED AWAY.

MMMFF!

NARRATOR: And so poor Hua tuo was killed by an impatient patient. It only goes to prove that medicine can be murder!

(CURTAIN FALLS)

It certainly can! Wait till you see what happens to the miserable measly medics in the next chapter. They really are doctors in danger… Do you fancy having a go at this perilous profession?

HOW TO BE A DOCTOR (without getting killed!)

So you want to be a doctor? Well, I'm sorry but that means you'll have to go back to school – medical school, that is. Let's face the facts…

Measly medicine fact file

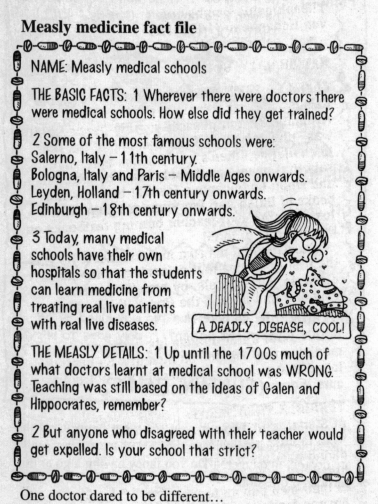

NAME: Measly medical schools

THE BASIC FACTS: 1 Wherever there were doctors there were medical schools. How else did they get trained?

2 Some of the most famous schools were:
Salerno, Italy – 11th century.
Bologna, Italy and Paris – Middle Ages onwards.
Leyden, Holland – 17th century onwards.
Edinburgh – 18th century onwards.

3 Today, many medical schools have their own hospitals so that the students can learn medicine from treating real live patients with real live diseases.

A DEADLY DISEASE, COOL!

THE MEASLY DETAILS: 1 Up until the 1700s much of what doctors learnt at medical school was WRONG. Teaching was still based on the ideas of Galen and Hippocrates, remember?

2 But anyone who disagreed with their teacher would get expelled. Is your school that strict?

One doctor dared to be different…

MEASLY MEDIC FILES

NAME: Paracelsus (Well, that's what he called himself. His real name was Philippus Aureolus Theophrastus Bombastus von Hohenheim (1493–1541) – well, you did ask!)

NATIONALITY: Swiss

CLAIM TO FAME: Paracelsus means "equal to Celsus" (he was a famous Roman medic, remember?). You guessed it – big-headed Phil was "phil" of himself. He was one of the first to challenge Galen's goofy ideas. Paracelsus said that people could only learn by experience and when he became a teacher he burnt the books of Galen and ibn Sina (see page 43). Just imagine your teacher burning textbooks on the first day of term!

Paracelsus had his own medical ideas. He was the first to realize that poisoning could cause diseases, for example, by breathing metal vapours. And he was the first to think of using chemicals as medicines.

DODGY DOC: Unfortunately his favourite medicine was the poison mercury. So having found that poison made people ill, he tried to cure them with more poison!

TERRIBLE TREATMENT: At Stertzing in 1534 he tried to cure plague by giving patients a tasty bread pill with a blob of their own poo on top. Anyone feeling peckish?

OPEN WIDE AND I'LL **PLOP** IT IN!

DON'T MENTION: Other doctors. Phil was always making fun of other doctors for their measly medical mistakes. So not surprisingly he was often chased out of towns by furious physicians. Phil died suddenly and it's said his enemies beat him up to teach him a lesson. Or was this just a measly rumour?

LET'S GIVE HIM A TASTE OF HIS OWN MEDICINE!

Loathsome laws

Every country made laws for doctors. Here are some from ancient Babylon (present-day Iraq).

THE LAWS OF KING HAMMURABI
(1792–1750 BC)

1. A DOCTOR WHO SAVES A LIFE GETS A REWARD IN SILVER. THE REWARD DEPENDS ON HOW IMPORTANT THE PATIENT IS. YOU DON'T GET TOO MUCH FOR A SLAVE.

2. A DOCTOR WHO BOTCHES AN OPERATION SO THAT A NOBLEMAN LOSES HIS EYE MUST HAVE HIS HAND CUT OFF.

So would you try your hand at surgery? Better not! In those days a surgeon had to practise surgery to keep their hand in!

In a few modern medical schools, new doctors still swear an oath to follow rules laid down by superdoc Hippocrates. It's called the Hippocratic Oath. I wonder if Dr Grimgrave swore it in ancient Greek times?

40

Grr — I swore a modern version if you must know!

Puzzling promises quiz

Here are ten promises. Four of them have never been part of the Hippocratic Oath and six have appeared in at least one version that doctors have sworn over the years. Which are the six genuine promises?

1. I will honour my teacher as much as my own parents.
2. I won't be scared to tell my teacher when they're wrong.
3. I will teach my teacher's children for nothing.
4. I won't perform cruel experiments on cuddly creatures.
5. I won't harm a patient.
6. I won't give out bad advice or dangerous drugs.
7. I'll always have a neat haircut and shiny shoes.
8. I won't tell stupid jokes.
9. I won't tell anyone my patients' secrets.
10. I won't do surgical operations.

Not all doctors lived up to their word, but many of the best did and what's more they genuinely tried to heal their patients – it wasn't their fault that their medical ideas were measly. And can you believe it? Some doctors were even kind and caring people...

THE NOT SO ^MEASLY MEDIC FILES

NAME: John Lettsom (1744–1815)

NATIONALITY: British (born in West Indies)

CLAIM TO FAME: One of the good guys of medicine

NOT-SO-DODGY DOC: When John was 23 he inherited an estate in the West Indies. It would have made him rich but the land was worked by slaves. John didn't agree with slavery so he set the slaves free and gave them the land. Instead he became a doctor in London and organized free medical aid for poor people.

NOT-SO-TERRIBLE TREATMENT: John believed in fresh air, sunshine and keeping clean. And he was right!

DON'T MENTION: After giving all his money to good causes, John fell on hard times. He had to sell his house and his books.

But other doctors suffered a far worse fate than John Lettsom. Let's find out why...

Docs in danger

Even dedicated docs could end up in trouble when they got mixed up in the perilous world of politics. Here are two physicians who fell foul of the powers that be...

Hall of fame: Abu Ali al-Husain ibn Abdallah ibn Sina (Known in Europe as Avicenna)

(AD 980–1037) Nationality: Born in present-day Uzbekistan

"ABU" GOT A LADDER?

Ibn Sina was the kind of kid who was so brainy that he learnt books off by heart for fun and when he studied medicine as a teenager he said it was "not difficult". When ibn Sina cured the local ruler his reward wasn't a bag of gold or even a bag of sweets – it was the chance to read the books in the palace library. Now that's a bit strange because there weren't any Horrible Science books to read then!

Not surprisingly, since he was an expert on everything, ibn Sina loved teaching and wrote books about astronomy, maths, music, religion, and philosophy. But his most famous work is called the Qanun and is a massive medical tome (that's a very big book). In fact, it was so big you could even use it as a tome-stone!

The book was packed with everything you could ever want to know about diseases and cures – and naturally Dr Grimgrave's read it from cover to cover...

Ibn Sina thought that the measles rash was mother's blood that had been trapped in a child before it was born. What a rash idea! But he was right to think TB spreads from person to person and that worms in the guts cause disease. I suppose he had a gut instinct, ha ha!

Yeah, he was no bonehead!

Ibn Sina's brainy book was read by doctors for the next 500 years. And no, that isn't how long it took to read.

Ibn Sina wandered from town to town teaching, but at last he settled in Hamadan. When he cured the local ruler he was made Prime Minister, but the ruler's soldiers turned against the doc. He was sacked and thrown into jail. Was this the end for the devoted doc?

NO! As luck would have it the ruler fell ill. When ibn Sina again cured the poorly prince, he got his job back. After the ruler died, the dynamic doc set off on his travels again – but his lively lifestyle wore him out. When his friends urged him to take it easy, he said:

I prefer a short life with width to a long life with length.

He fell ill and found the only person he couldn't heal was himself.

Now here's our second tale of a doctor in danger... Right now he's on the run.

ESCAPED PRISONER REPORT
By the Holy Inquisition 7 April 1553

NAME: Michael Servetus

KNOWN FACTS: Servetus escaped from prison just as we were about to burn him for his barmy beliefs. What a spoilsport!

He missed the "big match"

KNOWN HABITS: Servetus is a doctor. He studied in France, where he discovered that blood flows from the heart to the lungs and back again. Grr – what do we care! If we catch Servetus we'll make his blood flow all right – out of his body!

KNOWN HAUNTS: Servetus is believed to be making for Geneva, Switzerland, the home of that equally notorious enemy of our Church, John Calvin.

Servetus's "crime" was to have his own ideas about the Christian religion. The religious leader John Calvin hated the people who wanted to burn Servetus. So he gave the desperate doctor a warm welcome? Yeah right – if you believe that you'll believe anything!

Calvin hated Servetus's ideas too. In fact the doctor was dotty to go to Geneva. Cruel Calvin had him arrested and thrown into a cell with no light, no heat and no toilet. On 27 October 1553 miserable Mike was tied to a stake and burnt alive. I bet he wasn't fired with enthusiasm…

THIS ISN'T THE WARM WELCOME I EXPECTED!

Test your teacher
Why not tie your teacher to a stake and ask them the following horribly hard question…

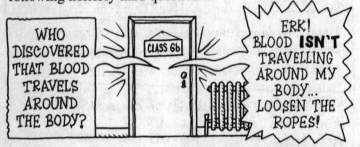

WHO DISCOVERED THAT BLOOD TRAVELS AROUND THE BODY?

CLASS 6b

ERK! BLOOD **ISN'T** TRAVELLING AROUND MY BODY… LOOSEN THE ROPES!

I'll give you a clue – it *wasn't* Servetus. He only found out how blood circles between the heart and the lungs. Any teacher worth their pay ought to know that English doc William Harvey (1578–1657) made the bloody breakthrough. But don't let your teacher off so easily, our doctor-god pal Imhotep may have known that blood moves around the body 4,500 years earlier.

More dodgy doctors
So you've trained at medical school and sworn the Hippocratic Oath? Great – now you're a fully fledged

physician! But get this – you didn't have to bother! Until Victorian times you could be a doctor with little or no medical training. Of course other docs *might* try to stop you. But often they didn't – as long as they made a living (whilst their patients made a dying) they weren't too bothered about boring old qualifications.

British doctors didn't have to be properly qualified by law until 1858. In that year only one-third of them actually had the right certificates – DISGRACEFUL!

Talk about lazy bones!

Today, the law is much tougher and it's really rare for people with no medical training to pretend to be doctors – but it still happens…

The Canada News

– June 1951 –

HAIL THE HERO HEALER!

All Canada is talking about Dr Joseph Cyr, the navy hero! After a raid off the enemy coast of North Korea, Dr Cyr saved the lives of three of our brave fighters. Said ship's captain James Plover, "Joe Cyr is a real fearless physician, and what's more he pulled out my bad tooth – I'm still waiting for the tooth fairy, though!"

But as they say, the tooth well out. Er, sorry, I mean TRUTH will out!

The Medical Times
-October 1951-

PHONEY PHYSICIAN FOUND OUT!

Joseph Cyr is a phoney fake! The hoaxing healer was unmasked when the real Dr Cyr's mum read newspaper stories about the man who's posing as her son. Today the Medical Times can reveal that the impostor is really a monk named Fred Waldo Demera. Dodgy Demera has never been to medical school in his life.

It looks like he's picked up a real bad habit!

Fred Waldo Demera

STOP PRESS
Fraudster Fred isn't even a proper monk. He's spent his whole life in jobs he's not trained to do. He's been a monk, a teacher, and a prison warden. Huh – the only job he's qualified for is a jailbird!

Oh, I don't know – being a prison warden sounds an excellent training for a teacher. Mind you, some people had to disguise themselves to stand *any* chance of becoming doctors. So who were they? I'll tell you in the next chapter!

WRETCHED WOMEN DOCTORS

Yes, I'm talking about *women*. And they were wretched because for hundreds of years, women were banned from being doctors.

Even hip Hippocrates wouldn't teach girls, although he did let them train as midwives (medics who help with births).

Four ways to get into medicine if you happened to be a girl

1 You could become a midwife. In Hippo's time, as now, they were mostly women.

2 You could be a Chinese doc at the time of the Song dynasty (10th–13th century). Rich women saw female doctors.

3 You could enrol at Salerno Medical School in the 11th century. You might even have a woman teacher named Trotula.

4 You could be a nun. Nuns nursed sick people and German nun Hildegard von Bingen (1098–1179) wrote a book about herbal remedies.

But apart from that, girls didn't get many chances to be doctors. No wonder trained female physicians were as rare as tap-dancing camels – and no wonder some fearless females dressed up as blokes just to get trained!

A special message to all girls reading this book... Just imagine you had to pretend to be a boy to get into science lessons! You might even have to dress in your brother's smelly old clothes...

HERE YOU ARE, SIS!

NO WAY!

Well, then – you've got to respect these…

Fighting female physicians

Ancient Greek Agnodice from Athens (3rd century BC) disguised herself as a lad to study medicine. When challenged by male docs Aggie owned up to being a woman and was put on trial. The penalty was DEATH. It was an open and shut case – after all, Aggie couldn't deny she was female, could she?

But then something amazing happened. Agnodice's women patients came to the trial. They protested that they wanted a woman to examine them and they forced the judges to spare Aggie and let women study medicine.

PHEW!

Well, that's the story anyway, but Dr Grimgrave doesn't believe a word of it...

Well, that's what boring old experts say – but even if they're right and Agnodice's story is just a legend, one woman really did make it as a doc in disguise. Her name was James Barry (1795–1865) – or that's what she called herself. Let's dig up the truth...

It's true! Britain's top army doc was a woman. Her real name was Miranda Barry. Helped by friends, brave Barry disguised herself as a boy to learn medicine. And she went on wearing trousers for the rest of her life.

But girls, maybe you want to become a doc without having to act like a brainless boy and using their smelly loos and burping in public? Well now you can, thanks to a fearless former teacher from the USA – Elizabeth Blackwell (1821–1910).

Elizabeth vowed to become a doctor after watching her best friend die of disease. Her friend begged to see a woman doctor but there weren't any. Elizabeth applied to go to medical school. They turned her down – because she was a woman. School after school turned her down – a dozen in all. At last, in 1847, battling Blackwell started lessons at Geneva Medical College, USA. She had only been allowed in after a vote by the students – and they had thought it was a joke!

At first the local people – and even some doctors – were so startled at the idea of a woman medic that they wouldn't talk to Elizabeth. But her determination and hard work won them over and in 1848 she finished her course and became America's first woman doctor. She had come top of her class.

I AM THE BEST WOMAN DOCTOR IN THE USA!

SHE'S THE **ONLY** WOMAN DOCTOR IN THE USA.

It took time for fuddy-duddy stick-in-the-mud male medics to get used to female doctors. At one British hospital, male students banned Elizabeth Garrett

Anderson (1836–1917) from medical classes because she could answer the teacher's questions and they couldn't. Girls weren't allowed to become doctors in Britain until 1876.

TODAY WOMEN DOCTORS WORK IN NEARLY EVERY COUNTRY. I SUPPOSE I'LL HAVE TO GET USED TO THEM.*

HI!

*We apologize for Dr G's out-of-date views.

Mind you, it doesn't really matter if your doc is a man, a woman or an alien from the Planet Blurb – they're only as good as their treatments. And hundreds of years ago you might live to regret paying your doctor a visit. Then again you might not live to regret anything!

MY TREATMENT SHOULD HAVE WORKED BY NOW. HOW LONG SINCE YOUR LAST VISIT?

ABOUT SIX MONTHS, DOCTOR.

"TERRIBLE TREATMENTS"

It's 300 years ago and you're feeling a bit off-colour. You decide to see a doctor. OH DEAR – BIG MISTAKE!

Measly diagnosis

The doctor starts by asking you questions. Sound familiar? Well, not quite – the doctor asks about your symptoms and takes your pulse, but he doesn't examine your body. Instead he takes a revoltingly close interest in your wee (that's urine if you want to sound like Dr Grimgrave).

"URINE" FOR A WEE TEST, YOUNG MAN!

I expect Dr Grimgrave thinks this is a load of rubbish...

Not necessarily! One can diagnose diseases such as blackwater fever from the colour of the patient's urine. A bad smell may be caused by infection and a sweet taste could be the result of a disease called diabetes. Of course, today we breed the germs and study them under a microscope — it's far more hygienic!

SPLOOSH!

So that's why old-time doctors sniffed or even tasted a patient's wee. Mind you, some doctors got their patients to do the job for them...

What's that? You've always wanted to test wee? Great! Here's a wee experiment you might like to try...

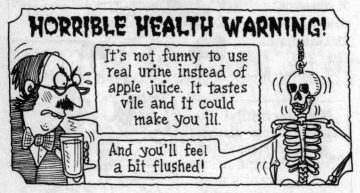

Dare you discover ... how to be a wee doctor

You will need:

3 glasses – labelled A, B and C.

Apple juice (ideally the cloudy variety). Well, what did you think we were going to use?

Sugar

A measuring jug

A teaspoon

Some understanding friends

Red food colouring

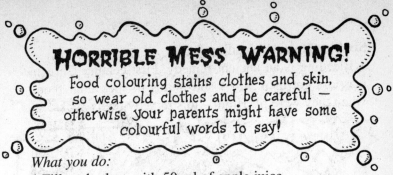

What you do:

1 Fill each glass with 50 ml of apple juice.

2 Add 200 ml of warm water to each glass.

3 Add 2–3 drops of red food colouring to glass A. This is blood, if anyone asks.

4 Add 2 teaspoonfuls of sugar to glass B and stir well.

5 Invite your friends to a wee-tasting session and challenge them to say which is the healthy wee.

WEE MUST BE POTTY!

You should find:

Your friends will have no difficulty in deciding that glass C is the healthy wee. But are they brave enough to try the test to begin with?

Meanwhile, back at ye olde doctor's, your potty pee physician has diagnosed your disease from your wee. That's the good news – the bad news is that he still believes in the awful ancient idea of humours and reckons yours are out of balance (see page 27). And the *really* measly news is that he wants to bleed you better!

Six bloodthirsty bleeding facts

1 Bleeding is an ancient remedy. First-century German warriors got their wives and mums to suck their blood when they were ill. Hmm – this remedy really sucks!

I VANT MY MUMMY!

TOUGH! YOU'RE MARRIED TO ME NOW!

2 On the Pacific island of Panape, people used sharks' teeth to let out "bad blood" from a patient. They thought it was "no fin" to worry about.

THERE'S SOMETHING FISHY ABOUT THIS TREATMENT...

3 By the 18th century measly medics in Europe and America were bleeding patients like there was no tomorrow – which was often true for the patients. The dangerous doctors often took 900 ml of blood – well, that's a bleeding liberty. Today blood donors aren't allowed to give more than 568 ml every *three months*.

4 The most common method of bleeding was to cut into a vein, but sometimes bloodsucking leeches were used (see page 60). And some doctors raised blisters with hot cups and then sliced them open… Fancy a nice hot cup of something?

5 Bleeding was used for every ailment you can imagine and quite a few you can't. In 1764 a maid swallowed a piece of toast the wrong way and it got stuck. She was bled.

6 Most bleeding was about as sensible as opening a shoe shop for slugs, but bleeding did seem to help the odd patient, as Dr Grimgrave will explain…

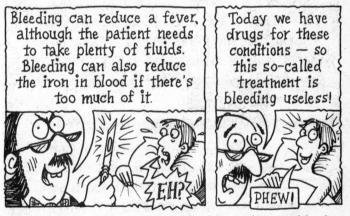

So how about you, readers? Would you let ye olde doc help himself to your blood? Well, if you're a little bleeder here's a little friend to help you part with the red stuff. Let's say hi to Hiru, the educated leech!

Good day, readers!
My name's actually Hirudo
medicinalis in Latin and
I'm a bloodthirsty
character. It's nothing
personal - I'm just
making a living. Back in
the good old days doctors put
me in a wine glass and held me against
the patient. Well, I do enjoy a little drink,
so I helped myself for 15 minutes and
then took a nap. Meanwhile the patients
were whining - I can't think why!

I wasn't fussy - I treated rich and
poor alike. Some poor people even used
to jump in my pond to get bled. And I
didn't charge them a penny! Is that
generosity or what? But I'm that kind
of caring creature!

And I never complained. The doctors
treated eye problems by making
me squirm up a patient's nose.
I treated rotten teeth by
wriggling into the patient's
mouth - but no one heard
a squeak out of me. I
guess I had plenty of

patience with my patients. Of course, some of them did take advantage of me - but then I'm a bit of a sucker at times! Anyway, all this chat has made me thirsty. Could you spare a drop of blood for a thirsty leech? Oh go on! Don't be shy! Hey, stop running away! Come back - pleeeeze! We can do lunch together!

It's OK, readers, I've plopped the leech back in his pond, so you can stop screaming now. Anyway, if you don't fancy being bled, your doctor has plenty more ruthless remedies to offer you. And they all have one thing in common...

THEY'RE USELESS!

I'd like to try them but I've got no body to take them with.

YE OLDE RUTHLESS REMEDY QUIZ

Can you work out which remedy was used for each patient's problem?

1 Patient is half-drowned.
a) Throw them back into the water and tell them to swim this time.
b) Stick a bellows up their backside and blow tobacco smoke.
c) Play them relaxing music.

2 Patient has typhus.
(a fever spread by lice).
a) Dip their feet in
honey and bird seed
and let pigeons peck
the patient's feet.
That'll give them a
clean bill of health!
b) Get the pigeons to
eat the lice.
c) Place the patient in a large oven
and cook them gently for a few hours.

3 Patient has yellow fever.
a) Feed them on bananas and custard.
b) Don't feed them for a month.
c) Sneak up behind them and throw
a bucket of water over them.

4 Patient has gout –
remember that painful
disease from page 11?
a) Cut off their
painful toe.
b) Dip their toe in
melted toffee.
c) Make them drink
2–3 glasses of cow's
wee every day.

5 Patient has the plague.
a) Force them to eat a rat, followed
by a cat.

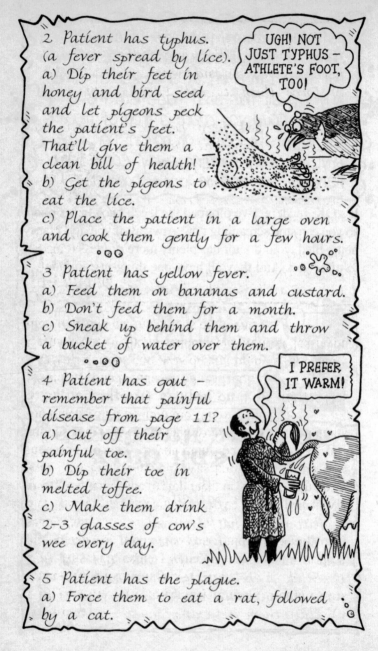

UGH! NOT JUST TYPHUS – ATHLETE'S FOOT, TOO!

I PREFER IT WARM!

b) Force them to eat dried human flesh served with some rather tasty herbs, olive oil and wine.
c) Force them to eat 1,999 prunes.

6 Patient has been cut by a sword.
a) Make them eat rust.
b) Grind up an Egyptian mummy, earthworms, pig brains and moss from the skull of a hanged man and smear it on the cut.
c) Do the same as b) but smear it on the sword.

OR d) – GET A BANDAGE!

Answers:

1 b) This was an 18th-century remedy. It didn't work – but then smoking is bad for you!

2 a) This 17th-century remedy was equally useless, although if you tried c) too you could bake a jolly tasty seed cake.

3 c) Tried in Haiti in the 1790s. To be fair the patient was also given lemonade to stop them drying out with fever.

4 c) This French remedy was known as "water of a thousand flowers". If you didn't have a cow you were supposed to drink your own wee. YUCK! If you drank too much you'd be a bit too full of yourself!

5 b) Suggested by Oswald Croll in 1609. This treatment sounds rather croll, er, cruel...

6 c) This curious cure was dreamt up by 17th-century German doc Wilhelm Hilden. Oh well, at least you didn't have to eat the odious ointment.

Charlie's cruel cures

In 1685 King Charles II of Britain fell ill. The king had a stroke and he would have died anyway, but he was given every medical treatment his doctors could think of … poor man!

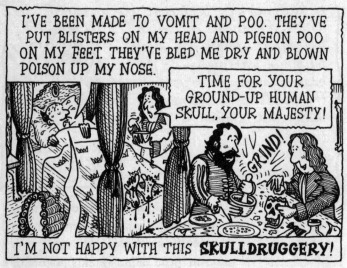

Anyway, you get the picture. Most ye olde measly medicines were as useful as a snake's hairdressing salon. No wonder lots of people gave up on medicine and turned to quacks…

But not that sort of quack!

Here's Dr Grimgrave to introduce this chapter…

A quack is someone who claims to have medical knowledge but has none. No wonder their treatments in this chapter were useless! You won't be hearing any wise quacks from me!

And I wouldn't be seen dead trying them!

In Victorian times American quacks would often sell their queasy quack remedies from the back of a wagon in small towns. If you wanted to do this you'd need…

1 A wagon.

2 A circus show to pull in the customers. A muscleman would be good – you could pretend his muscles developed after trying your remedy.

3 Some medicine to sell – coloured water will do fine.

4 Fast horses to get you out of town before your customers realize they've been conned.

PAH! THIS IS JUST WATER!

ER… WELL… YES, B-B-BUT NOT JUST ANY OLD WATER… IT'S, ER, RED WATER!

TIME TO GO

It all sounds deeply dodgy and completely crooked. So which quack treatment would you waste your hard-earned pocket money on?

Horrible Healthcare presents...
COMPLETELY CURIOUS CURES

Treat yourself to our quirky quack treatments!
You'll find they really pay off!
(Well, we'll get paid off anyway!)

Joanna Stephens's bladder - stone cure (1738)
So what's in it? Just pay £3,000 and all will be revealed. Clue — it'll come out in the wash!

GET DOWN TO EARTH WITH **James Graham's amazing earth baths** (1780s). You get buried up to your neck in earth! You'll live to be 100 and what's more it's dirt cheap — er, no it isn't.

ARE YOU GREEN AROUND THE GILLS?
You'll be dying to try **Samuel Thomson's healthy herbal remedies** (1800s). Ideal for anyone with green fingers!
The small print - you could be green all over afterwards!

EEK! WE'RE OUTA HERE!

NEED A BUZZ?

Try **William A. Bailey's Radithor** (1925). It contains genuine radium — it's so radioactive you can listen to your favourite radio programme!

UNDER THE WEATHER?

Check out what's bugging you with **Dr Albert Abrams' dynomizer** (1923). Just send Dr A some dried blood and he'll use his marvellous machine to diagnose what's wrong with you. All the fun of finding out you've got a deadly disease! If you're lucky you might have a disease that doctors haven't heard of!

ARE YOU GETTING ENOUGH ZZZZZ?

You will with new **1950s-style Z water** — it's water with added Z rays — so it's sure to put that extra ZZZZZZ-ip into your life!

Six sickening secrets that the Horrible Healthcare people absent-mindedly forgot to tell you…

1 In 1738 rich people and the British Parliament paid sneaky Stephens £3,000 for her rotten remedy. But the measly medicine was mostly eggshells and soap. People still tried it and British Prime Minister Robert Walpole ended up eating over 81 kg of soap. It didn't cure his bladder stones – but I bet he could blow brilliant bubbles!

SHHH! HE'S SLEEPING!

2 James Graham (1745–1794) later went mad and ended up being buried in earth himself (but he was dead by then)!
3 US quack Samuel Thomson (1769–1843) used poisonous plants in his horrible herbal remedies. When one of his followers tried the treatment on a British woman she died. The name of the killer quack? Al Coffin, of course!

GREEN HERBAL REMEDY.

SAMUEL THOMSON'S HERBAL REMEDY

GREEN PATIENT.

4 Radioactive means that the substance gives off invisible high-energy rays that can kill you, not make you better. US tycoon Eben McBurney Byers (1868–1927) drank over 1,000 bottles of radithor. It killed him in a revolting way – his bones broke, his skin developed sores and holes appeared in his skull. Poor Eben – he was dying to get better but he ended up dying!

5 A scientist sent Dr Abrams a blood sample and he diagnosed a long list of deadly diseases. What dodgy Dr A didn't know was that the blood came from a chicken – what a fowl trick! He should have diagnosed chickenpox.

6 Z water turned out to be strangely similar to tap water and the crooked-cure sellers went to jail.

So what could you do if your quack remedy proved to be a dead duck? Well, you could try a few folklore remedies. (Folklore means traditional knowledge that gets passed down by word of mouth.) Some of them were guaranteed to end your suffering … that's end it for ever!

Here is an old book of remedies from Dr Grimgrave's granny.

Granny Grimgrave's Book of Health

Granny knows best, my dears, and Granny says good health is very important. In fact it's so important it's worth dying for!

Chapter 1 ~ PREVENTION IS BETTER THAN CURE

The best cure is not to get ill. I swear by my lucky health charm. It was given to me by an Apache medicine man and it's guaranteed to work ... like a charm!

TEETH FROM A DEAD ENEMY

PIECE OF JAWBONE FOR EXTRA GOOD LUCK

Chapter 2 ~ A CHILLED CHILD IS A HEALTHY CHILD

I'm a tough old granny and that's why I use the traditional 18th-century method to toughen up children. Every morning you duck them in an ice-cold bath. Leave their windows open in winter and make sure their clothes and socks are soaking. You'll save money on heating and the children can pretend to be ice sculptures.

VRRRRRRRRR!

DEAD HEALTHY

Urgent note to parents ...
DO NOT TRY THIS AT HOME! 18th-century bookseller
George Nicol tried it on five of his children ... and they all died!

Chapter 3 ~ ACHES AND PAINS

Aches can be a pain in the bottom (and other places), but Granny knows how to get rid of them. All you need to do is rub a mole's paw on them. If you've got toothache why not chase a cat across a ploughed field and rub its sweaty bottom on your teeth?

THE TOOTHACHE'S GONE BUT NOT THE TASTE OF CAT BOTTOM!

If the cat scratches you can always try an old Scottish wound remedy. Cut the cat's ear and let its blood drip on your painful bits. Of course the cat might be upset

HOW ARE YOUR EARS?

EH?

about its own painful bits but you can always plop warm dung on them – your cat will soon be feline fine! And if you or your cat has earache you can treat it the old Irish way – boil a cockroach in oil and stuff it in the ear hole.

Chapter 4 ~ COLOURFUL COLD CURES

Colds can be a misery but Granny knows some sure–fire cures! Wrap yourself in red flannel cloth and you won't be off–colour! And if that doesn't work, put a dog in your bed and plop a live fish into your mouth. One of them will catch your cold and you'll feel a lot better! Now that's what I call creature comforts!

YOUR CURES ARE A PAIN IN THE NECK.

MOLE'S PAW

GRANNY WILL RUB IT BETTER!

There's something fishy about that last cure – it could be even be a shaggy dog tail! But the really stunning fact about foul folklore is that some of it actually worked!

Bet you never knew!

1 In England and the Ukraine, country people traditionally put mouldy bread on wounds. And they weren't just loafing about because in 1928 scientists found the germ-killing antibiotic penicillin in mould juice (see page 134 for more manky details).

FESTER!

IT'S A ROTTEN REMEDY... BUT IT WORKS!

2 One thousand years ago in China people blew dried pustules from smallpox scabs up children's noses. And no, this wasn't some kind of Chinese child torture. Coming into contact with weak smallpox germs helped the children's white blood cells learn how to fight the full-blown disease. In Turkey, old women stuck needles dripping with pus from smallpox victims into the arms of healthy people for the same reason.

72

Scientists have been testing traditional treatments for years. People in southern Italy thought you could cure a tarantula spider's bite with a dance called the tarantella. They thought that animals tried to dance when they get bitten, so scientist Giorgio Baglivi (1669–1707) decided on an experiment…

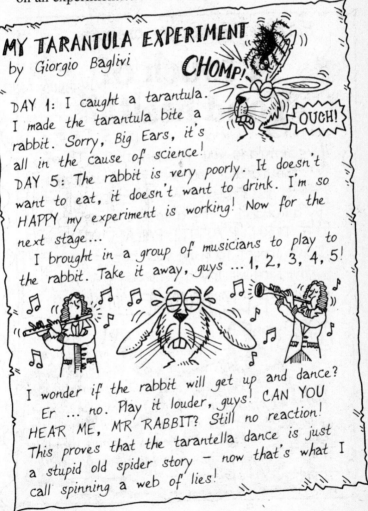

MY TARANTULA EXPERIMENT
by Giorgio Baglivi

CHOMP!

OUCH!

DAY 1: I caught a tarantula. I made the tarantula bite a rabbit. Sorry, Big Ears, it's all in the cause of science!

DAY 5: The rabbit is very poorly. It doesn't want to eat, it doesn't want to drink. I'm so HAPPY my experiment is working! Now for the next stage…

I brought in a group of musicians to play to the rabbit. Take it away, guys … 1, 2, 3, 4, 5!

I wonder if the rabbit will get up and dance? Er … no. Play it louder, guys! CAN YOU HEAR ME, MR RABBIT? Still no reaction! This proves that the tarantella dance is just a stupid old spider story — now that's what I call spinning a web of lies!

OK, so you knew the experiment wouldn't work – but it was an early example of scientists being, well, scientific about medicine. Today all treatments are tested before anyone is allowed to try them and it's easy to see which ones don't work. But here's a useless treatment you might want to try anyway – it really does pay off…

If your cures killed you there was a final service you could offer science. You could let doctors dissect (that's cut up) your body. So you don't fancy being sliced on a slab? Well that's tough! A gang of savage surgeons will dig you up anyway!

YIKES – I'M FEELING RATTLED!

75

DREADFUL DISSECTION

Dr Grimgrave has a dark and dreadful secret. On some nights he creeps into the basement of his local hospital … and cuts up dead bodies. But DON'T PANIC, READERS – Dr G isn't a mad scientist! Well, not that mad, anyway…

Now cutting up a dead body isn't everyone's cup of tea (in fact it's not a good idea to have your tea whilst you're doing it). So would you like to try it? Whilst you're deciding, here's a true story to show you just how scary it can be…

Are *you* brave enough?

Lancaster, England, 1820

The November evening had long since turned to night as I stood shivering in front of the castle prison. Nervously my mind slid back to the horrors of the afternoon. And the horrible sights I'd seen within these very walls…

I remembered following my employer, old Mr Dickson, across the cobbled courtyard to the old tower. Up the winding staircase we climbed, to a cold, bare room. This was the prison washroom – and the morgue.

Here the bodies lay under white sheets waiting for Mr Dickson to cut them up and find out what killed them.

"They'll do you no harm, Richard," said Mr Dickson gently. "If you want to be a doctor you have to be prepared for grisly sights. So the question is, lad, are you brave enough?"

"Er, I think so," I stammered.

He flung back a sheet...

I gasped. I was looking at the face of a young prisoner I'd tried to treat last week. Now the young man was dead and his face was grey and ghastly. With mounting horror, I watched Mr Dickson raise his knife and begin to cut open the body...

Now I was back. The grim castle walls seemed to reach the stormy ink-black clouds. I clutched the bottle of medicine Mr Dickson had given me to deliver and thought about the private mission I had set myself. Would I be brave enough? I took a deep breath and grasped the great cold iron knocker, letting it fall with a dead, heavy thud. My heart thudded as hard as the doorknocker.

After a while the huge iron-studded door creaked open.

"Oh it's you, young master Richard," said the jailer. "You've brought the medicine, I suppose."

He didn't blink as I asked to visit the morgue. He simply handed me a lantern and a large, cold key. I suppose he thought I had a job to do up there for Mr Dickson.

Scarcely daring to breathe, I picked my way across the dark and windy courtyard towards the tower. My heart was pounding now, but I knew I had to go there.

"I've got to prove I can do it," I told myself grimly. "I'm going to see grisly sights as a doctor. The question is – am I brave enough to face them alone?"

My teeth began to chatter.

As I turned the heavy key in the lock a sudden gust of air made me sway. The lantern door swung open and the light went out.

I placed the lantern on the ground. I would have to go there in the dark.

As I stepped inside the tower, the door slammed behind me with a bang. Darkness swallowed me up. Scarcely daring to breathe, I began to feel my way up the stairs to the place where the bodies were waiting. All I could hear was the wind howling and the air muttering and sighing through the windows. It sounded like the voices of ghosts.

"They can't hurt me," I whispered to myself.

Suddenly I stopped dead. My stomach turned to ice. Above me on the stairs stood a thin and ghastly shape with a face that I knew. It was the man from the slab. The man I had seen cut up. He was waiting for me…

With a cry of horror, I turned and tripped and stumbled back down the worn spiral stone stairs. Round and down, round and down I ran. But there was something – someone – below. A flash of white, a glimpse of another dead face. I was trapped! Something reached out and grasped my ankle with cold dead fingers. Panting loudly with terror, I reached down and touched it…

It was a white sheet.

All of a sudden I came to my senses. The moon had come out and was shining through the window at a sheet hanging from a nail to dry on the stairs. I hadn't noticed it in the dark. And what of the other ghost?

I took a deep ragged breath and gingerly made my way back up the stairs.

Yes, there it was! A patch of light on the wall. I must have imagined the face. I *must* have.

I sighed with relief. Shakily I turned once more and made my way from the tower of terror. I'd seen enough. A doctor has to be ready for grisly sights, but ghosts – well, that's something else.

So why do it?

You'll be delighted to hear that young Richard Owen decided that he was brave enough for dissection. In fact he loved it! He went to university and in time became the famous scientist who invented the word "dinosaur".

SHPLURRRP!

I WAS CUT OUT FOR THIS JOB!

But why does anyone want to cut up a body? We asked Dr Grimgrave…

Dissection is the best way to find out how a body is put together – this study is called anatomy. Surgeons need to practise their skills on patients who don't complain, ha ha.

We have to be dead patient…

Dissection is also needed to discover the cause of death. This is called a post-mortem. Doctors remove damaged or diseased organs* and preserve them for further study.

*organs = body parts such as the brain with a particular job to do.

Today doctors regularly train by dissecting bodies, but in the past things weren't so cut and dried.

The gory story of dissection cut up into neat slices

In places as far apart as ancient China, India, Greece and Rome, dissection was banned for religious reasons. And that meant our old pal Galen had to make do with apes, dogs, pigs and the odd elephant. No wonder his idea of anatomy was a bit hit and miss.

REPORT ON GALEN'S ANATOMY IDEAS

By Dr Grimgrave (trying to stay calm)

Galen believed...

1 Nerves take messages to and from the brain. The messages to the brain are our sense of touch and the messages from the brain order the muscles to work. They even control the voice.

> SPOT ON – ALTHOUGH THE MESSAGES TO THE BRAIN INCLUDE OUR OTHER SENSES TOO.

2 Air travels from the lungs to the heart where it meets the blood that has passed though tiny holes in the heart's wall.

> THIS IDEA IS FULL OF HOLES!

3 The blood vessels under the human brain are the same as those in a horse.

> NEIGH CHANCE!

Remember how docs thought Galen was right about disease? Well, they also thought that his was the last word on anatomy. So why didn't anyone dissect a body to prove him wrong? That was easier said than done. Cutting up bodies was still banned, and at medical school assistants did the rare dissections. Young doctors weren't encouraged to look for themselves. One teacher, Jacob Sylvius, said he thought that Galen was wrong but he believed this was because the body had changed since Roman times! It took a reckless robber to prove that the teachers and Galen were wrong...

The Horrible Science Silver Scalpel Awards for the Most Creative Body Cutter in History

1st Prize – Andreas Vesalius (1514–1564)

Nationality: Born in present-day Belgium

Claim to fame: Proved Galen wrong by stealing bodies and cutting them up for himself. Thanks to Vesalius, dissection became very popular with docs.

Praiseworthy feat: He wasn't scared to argue with his teachers. He told stupid Sylvius that he was only fit to hold a knife at the dinner-table. Of course, arguing with your teachers isn't always a sign of genius…

YOU'RE NOT FIT TO HOLD CHALK TO THE BLACKBOARD!

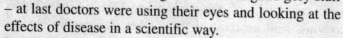

2nd Prize – Giovanni Morgagni (1682–1771)

Nationality: Italian

Claim to fame: Studied the effects of disease on the body's insides. When he was 80 he published a big book listing the effects of diseases on the body's organs. This was good gory stuff – at last doctors were using their eyes and looking at the effects of disease in a scientific way.

Praiseworthy feat: Proved the ancient docs wrong. Death was caused by damage to organs and not too much of a humour.

SILVER SCALPEL AWARD

3rd Prize – John Hunter (1728–1793)
Nationality: Scottish
Claim to fame: Dissected everything, including the Prime Minister (after he was dead). Hunter built up a museum of 14,000 human and animal body bits.
Praiseworthy feat: He was never scared to speak his mind. Even if it meant being rude…

HE MADE CUTTING REMARKS…

AT LAST – A DOCTOR I REALLY APPROVE OF!

So you want know what he said? Here's what John Hunter told a relative who stopped him from dissecting a body to find out what the person died of…

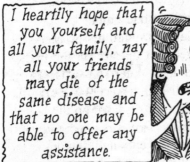

I heartily hope that you yourself and all your family, nay all your friends may die of the same disease and that no one may be able to offer any assistance.

NOW STEADY ON, OLD CHAP!

Well, talk about rude health! Could you be that rude – and if so, could you be a demon dissector? Here's your chance to find out!

Dreadful dissection quiz (Based on the life of John Hunter)

How to play
Each question has two sets of answers – a fairly normal one and an out-and-out revolting one. Which is correct?

1 How do you test stomach juices from dead bodies?
a) Sensible scientist   **b)** Demon dissector

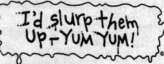

I'd test them using harmless chemicals.

I'd slurp them up – YUM YUM!

2 How do you strip the flesh from a skeleton?
a) Sensible scientist   **b)** Demon dissector

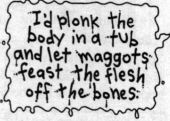

I'd bury it for 20 years and then dig it up.

I'd plonk the body in a tub and let maggots feast the flesh off the bones.

3 How do you get rid of leftover body bits?
a) Sensible scientist   **b)** Demon dissector

I'd give them a decent burial.

I'd make them into garden compost.

4 What is your final wish?
a) Sensible scientist   **b)** Demon dissector

To give my pupils the day off.

To be dissected by my pupils.

Awful answers:

SHOCK HORROR – *ALL* THE ANSWERS ARE B)!

1 b) Medical students did this – fancy a slurp?

2 b) And it was smelly.

3 b) This led to a riot when some boys found the body bits in a cart.

4 b) Would your teacher make the ultimate sacrifice to educate you?

After Hunter died visitors came to see his medical museum and it was then that the terrible truth dawned. Many of John Hunter's bodies had been stolen from their graves. This was a very grave matter…

Hunter certainly stole his prize exhibit. It was the skeleton of a giant that was supposed to be at the bottom of the sea. So how on Earth did he get hold of it?

The casebook of Chief Inspector Bone

THE MYSTERY OF THE GIANT'S BONES

Charles Byrne was a wonder to behold. He came from Ireland and stood 2.51 metres in his socks. In 1782, he came to London and people paid good money just to look at him. He was a really HUGE attraction.

HI!

John Hunter was one of these paying customers but he wanted more. Hunter wanted to dissect the giant's body. Within a short time Mr Byrne fell ill and lost all his money. And it was then that Mr Hunter made his offer. He would pay Mr Byrne for the right to cut up his body after he died. But Mr Byrne did not want to be dissected – in fact he felt really cut up about it. Mr Byrne begged his friends to throw his body into the sea so that it would be safe from Mr Hunter.

Mr Byrne's friends swore they carried out Mr Byrne's last wish. So how did Mr Byrne's bones end up in Mr Hunter's medical museum? Hmm – the case is still open even if the coffin lid is nailed shut...

HMMM TASTY!

So what happened?

a) John Hunter fished the body from the sea.

b) Horrible Hunter was desperate to get his hands on the giant's body. He bumped off Byrne and bribed his friends to say they had thrown the body in the sea.

c) Hunter bribed the undertaker to steal the body and trick the giant's friends.

Answer: c) The crooked undertaker got the friends drunk then he stole the body from the coffin and replaced it with rocks. Well, stone me!

HE WAS A GOOD FRIEND.

BUT HE'S STONE DEAD NOW.

AND HE'S DEAD HEAVY!

87

But some doctors went well beyond stealing bodies. They turned a blind eye to MURDER!

WANTED FOR MURDER!

William Burke and William Hare

Known haunts: Edinburgh, Scotland (1829)
Known crimes: Luring innocent victims to Hare's lodging house and then smothering them. They've killed at least 16 people and sold the bodies to Dr Robert Knox for his dissection classes.
Reward: Two VIP tickets to the execution!

Burke and Hare were cruel killers. They didn't care who they killed for cash. But their callous criminal careers ended when Burke's lodgers found the body of an old woman in the spare room. The police persuaded Hare to give evidence against Burke and 40,000 people turned up to see Burke's execution. Burke's body was cut up by the doctors but this time he didn't get payment – he got payback.

Bet you never knew!
1 Some of Burke's skin was used to bind a book. I guess that made him a "well-read" criminal.
2 Even though Dr Knox must have known about the murders, he was never charged with any crime. But he was so hated he had to leave Edinburgh for ever.

Shocked by these cruel crimes, the British government gave doctors the right to dissect any unwanted body. There was no more need for them to buy stolen corpses. At last the reign of terror was over … or was it?

Never say die?

In the past medicine was so measly that doctors weren't always too sure whether a person was dead or not.

In 1832 a tall Irish policeman died. The body was so big that the undertaker tried to break its legs to fit it in the coffin. He hit the body with a hammer – and it yelled! Or you could say the badly bashed bobby's body bawled and bounded back to life. Mind you, I bet the undertaker yelled even louder!

You'll be relieved to read that today dead people are tested very carefully to make sure they really are dead. But in the past it was quite possible for a not-quite-perished patient to be buried alive. It sounds DEAD scary – but there were even worse fates. Such as being cut up … alive!

In 1587 an executed criminal woke up when a surgeon stuck a knife in his chest. He lived a few days and then went back to being dead.

In 1740 a teenage boy was executed for stealing. Surgeons were just about to cut open his body when he coughed and sat up. He lived – and what's more he didn't get cut up.

That made him luckier than many victims of surgery. They were always alive and kicking when they were cut up. But they weren't quite so lively afterwards…

⋮SAVAGE ⋮SURGERY ⋮

Sorry, readers, Dr G wants to tell you a dreadful doctor joke…

Surgeons are really funny people — they leave their patients in stitches!

And some of them are right **sew and sews!**

It would be so much easier if humans were robots. That way a surgeon could be a mechanic who slots in a new battery or tightens a screw. But humans aren't machines. If you try to open them they feel, they bleed, they scream…

Savage surgeons and suffering soldiers
The most savage surgery happened on battlefields. After every fight there were mangled men for the surgeons to practise their kills on, er I mean practise their skills on – and I bet the men wished they'd died in the battle. After one battle at Borodino in 1812, French surgeon Dominique Jean Larrey (1766–1842) hacked off 200 legs. I bet Larrey felt hacked off at the end of the day, but he became a legend for his work. Mind you, battlefield surgery would have been even more savage if it wasn't for this man…

Hall of fame: Ambroise Paré
(1510–1590) Nationality: French
Ambroise once declared that a doctor should always hold out hope for his patient – even if there wasn't any. But when he started work as an army surgeon there wasn't

much hope for a soldier who had been shot. Doctors thought that gunpowder made wounds rot – of course this was a load of rot...

Gunpowder blasts germs into wounds of course these blasted doctors didn't know about germs.

They needed to bone up on the subject.

In those days doctors cut off wounded arms and legs and poured boiling oil over the stumps to stop the bleeding. That's what Paré did until one day in 1537 when he ran out of oil...

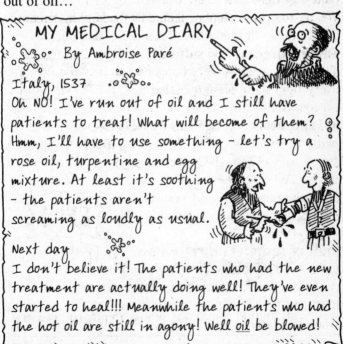

MY MEDICAL DIARY
By Ambroise Paré

Italy, 1537

Oh NO! I've run out of oil and I still have patients to treat! What will become of them? Hmm, I'll have to use something – let's try a rose oil, turpentine and egg mixture. At least it's soothing – the patients aren't screaming as loudly as usual.

Next day

I don't believe it! The patients who had the new treatment are actually doing well! They've even started to heal!!! Meanwhile the patients who had the hot oil are still in agony! Well oil be blowed!

91

The new mixture soothed the wounds and gave the body's own natural repair systems a chance to work. Ambroise made a momentous decision…

Quick queasy quiz

Which extra ingredients did Paré later add to his mixture? WARNING – it might have been more than one!

a) Custard

b) Puppy fat

c) Mashed-up worms

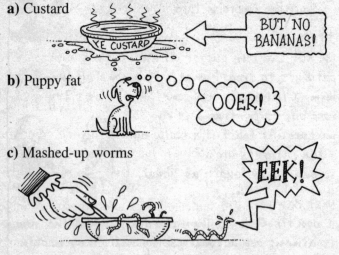

92

Paré became famous. One day he was captured and faced death but when the enemy found out who he was, he was released. In 1545 Paré wrote a book about his discoveries and his career as a superstar surgeon really took off.

He became the King's surgeon. When his pal King Henri II of France suffered a head injury Paré planned an op to save him. He practised the op on the chopped-off heads of executed prisoners and he had just got a-head of the problem when the King died.

Amazing Ambroise went on to invent artificial arms and legs and even false teeth. But in 1572 he found himself in a seriously savage situation. Supporters of King Charles IX had ordered the murder of all French Protestants and Ambroise belonged to this faith. As luck would have it, anxious Ambroise was with the King at the time. The King said:

It is not right that one who is worth a whole world of men should be murdered.

TOO RIGHT!

You might think it's not right to murder anyone – but at least the King hid the doctor in his own bedroom.

The putrid past

Despite the efforts of dedicated docs like Ambroise Paré, surgery still killed many patients. Like the doctors, surgeons were doing their best to save lives, but their best wasn't very good. And they had two fatal problems – pain and germs. Let's take a peek at the putrid past…

Savage surgery 1800-style

1 Surgeons were proud of their blood-encrusted aprons. **2** Surgeon's knife hasn't been washed. **3** Nor has the saw. **4** Nor has the thread to tie up blood vessels. **5** Some hospitals used handcuffs to stop patients running away. **6** Sand and shovel to mop up blood. **7** Box of sawdust for the leg. **8** Stove to heat hot irons (used to stop bleeding).

Those instruments and clothes are crawling with germs. The chances of death were about 1 in 3.

Mind you, Liston wasn't always so successful. One of his ops was the most bloody ever! Here's how it would have sounded on the radio. (Well, that's if they had radios in those days.) Cover your ears if you don't like grisly bits!

Welcome to Top of the Ops Live. My name's Mike Commentator and we're here to witness history being made. Today surgeon Robert Liston will be trying to break his own world cutting-off-the-leg speed record of 150 seconds...

And here comes Liston now. He's dressed in his usual blood-spattered green coat and Wellington boots. He's looking calm and relaxed — which is more than I can say for the patient!

Liston's calling for his assistant to time him. He's drawing his knife — it's got a notch in the handle for each of his previous ops. And he's off. He's cutting into the leg. The patient is struggling and

screaming. He's being held down as Liston slices around the bone ... OH MY GOODNESS! Liston's cut off three of his assistant's fingers. The knife must have slipped — it must have been all that blood. And it's sliced off a piece of patient too! Liston's pulled out the knife and — OH NO I don't believe it! He's cut the coat-tails off a spectator. The man's fainted — NO, HE'S DEAD! He's had a heart attack because he thought he'd been stabbed.

And now the operating theatre is in chaos! The blood is squirting everywhere, the patient is screaming, the assistant is screaming — I'm SCREAMING! But Liston

YARGH!

is sawing the bone and tying up the blood vessels as if nothing has happened. What a performer! But I'm sorry to say that Robert Liston has failed to break his world cutting-off-the-leg record. And now he's got to do it all another day! I guess he'll be looking for another patient to practise on!

NOT OVER MY DEAD BODY!

OR MINE!

OR MINE!

The patient and the assistant both died from infections caused by the surgery – making this the worst operation ever. It was the only op where three people got the chop.

A painful subject

What a painful story! And pain was the cause of the disaster. Liston made mistakes because he was in too much of a hurry. And he was rushing the op to keep the patient's pain to a minimum. So I guess he was killing with kindness.

In 200 BC Chinese surgeons were experimenting with herbs that put patients to sleep. European and American surgeons were more savage, though. They thought painkillers (or anaesthetics (an-ess-thet-icks) if you want to sound like an expert) were namby-pamby. They gave their patients alcohol or drugs such as opium to dull their senses – if they were lucky! Brutal British army doctor John Hall said…

It is much better to hear a fellow shouting with all his might than to see him sink quietly into his grave.

YEOW!

Good man!

Try quoting that to your teachers next time they tell you off for yelling!

A painful quiz

1 Some questions may have more than one right answer.
2 For each wrong answer you lose a point! I know it's hard but this quiz is meant to HURT!

1 The pain of ops limited the sort of things that surgeons in Europe could do. So what could they manage?
a) Heart transplants.
b) Tooth transplants.
c) Cutting out stones from the bladder.

2 Which of the following methods of pain control were tried by surgeons?
a) Banging the patient over the head with a large stick.
b) Insulting lady patients in a bid to make them faint.
c) Doings ops at night when the patient was asleep.

Answers:
1 b) Our old pal John Hunter pioneered tooth transplants. Poor children were paid a few pennies to have their teeth pulled out – then they were given to greedy rich people who ate too many sweets. And I'm sure you'll be pleased to read that the transplanted teeth dropped out after a few years.

1 c) Cutting out bladder stones was common – in fact French royal surgeon Clever de Maldigny even did the op on himself! Yes, readers, Clever was his name but don't try this at home – it's really not that Clever!
2 a) 18th-century dentist Martin van Butchell tried this.
2 b) French doc Baron Guillaume Dupuytren (1777–1835) tried this. (By the way this technique does NOT work on lady teachers.)

In the 1840s surgery began to get a little kinder … well, a tiny bit.

It's a knockout!

US doctors began to experiment with painkilling gas, and it's said that one of their first patients was a young woman named Alice Mahon. The story goes that in 1846 Alice had her leg cut off. But the ether gas supplied by William Morton (1819–1868) knocked her out. Here's what surgeon George Hayward said to Alice when she came round…

A dirty little problem

Soon surgeons all over Europe were using painkilling gases and you might think that surgery was set for a painless future. Well you would think that if you've forgotten about those gruesome operating-theatre germs. Patients still died of horrible hospital infections – but now they died a bit less painfully. We'll be getting to grips with germs on page 114 – but right now we're rushing into hospital…

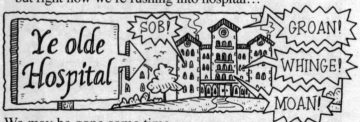

We may be gone some time…

Another dreadful doctor joke…

Why do hospital doctors walk in circles?

THEY'RE JUST DOING THEIR ROUNDS!

It doesn't tickle my funny bone.

Have you ever been into hospital? Hopefully it was a clean, well-run place. But 200 years ago, hospitals could be hell.

Horrible Healthcare presents…

The Ye Olde Hospital Experience

Come and experience life or death in a genuine ye olde hospital…
You'll make lots of new friends! You'll be sharing a bed with up to five people! Drunk and dirty nurses! Free disease-swap service!

I CAME IN WITH A SORE TOE BUT NOW I'VE GOT…

DIARRHOEA | CHOLERA | TYPHUS | AND FLEAS!

We won't let in anyone with the plague or leprosy – but anyone else is welcome to stay and give their bugs to the rest of us.

In the 18th century, ordinary hospitals were bad but mental hospitals were worse. In those days doctors didn't have a clue what caused diseases of the mind. Conditions were cruel and the treatments really took the biscuit – in fact they were plain crackers!

Cruel conditions and crazy cures

1 Prisoners, er sorry, patients at the Salpetriére Hospital in Paris were locked in dungeons that flooded with filthy river water. I suppose they ended up insane and in-Seine. And if that wasn't bad enough, they were often chewed by sewer rats.

2 That was luxury compared to London's hospitals. At Bethlem Hospital, a wretched man named James Norris was kept in chains for fifteen years – I guess doctors thought he was the weakest link. Meanwhile at the Bethnal Green madhouse a woman patient was tied up and thrown in a pigsty.

URGH!

LOOK, MUM! WE'VE GOT A VISITOR!

DON'T TELL PORKIES!

3 If you were a patient at Bethlem Hospital the nearest you got to fun was when heartless people paid to laugh at you. Well, they were having fun anyway. And at the Bicêtre Hospital in Paris patients even had to dance for visitors. It was either that or get a whipping.

4 Patients of US doctor Benjamin Rush (1745–1813) were strapped to this potty patient chair…

I WON'T STAND FOR THIS!

Box over patient's head so they can't bite anyone.

Patient tied to chair.

Potty for those little emergencies.

YOU WON'T GET A CHANCE!

And they had to sit there for *days* on end.

5 Another favourite treatment – well, it was a favourite with doctors anyway – was to sit the patient in a deep hot bath with a canvas cover to the keep the heat in. The heat soon exhausted the poor patient who was left to stew for days on end. If you tried this you really would be in hot water!

6 Many docs, such as German Johann Christian Reil (1759–1813), thought that nice hot baths were a bit too cosy. Ruthless Reil preferred to flog his patients with a leather whip and throw them into icy water. Isn't that a chilling thought?

Doctors probably thought they were being cruel to be kind, but their treatments sound kind of cruel. Let's hope your madhouse, er, school isn't this bad! Anyway, things could only get better and they did thanks to a tiny band of caring people.

A few good guys

In 1793 shy French doc Phillipe Pinel (1745–1826) became boss of the sinister Bicêtre Hospital. Pinel had no more idea how to treat diseases of the mind than anyone else. But he believed in using kindness and reason to bring patients to their senses. When he arrived he found many of the patients chained up, so he set them free. Some of them got better.

A man named Chevigne had been chained up for ten years. Pinel freed him. At this time revolution was raging in France and one day the doc was attacked by a mob that thought he was against the Revolution. The mob was about to hang Pinel when Chevigne showed up and chased them away. Oh well, one good turn deserves another!

GRRR, NOW YOU'VE REALLY **MADE ME MAD!**

Could you be a doctor?

You are Philippe Pinel. Lots of people are getting their heads chopped off in the Revolution. A tailor is so scared of it happening to him that he goes mad. I guess he lost his head about losing his head. What would you do?

a) Take him to a few executions and say, "There – that's not so bad is it?"

b) Order him to make everyone new clothes.

c) Dress up some doctors as judges. Pretend to put the tailor on trial and find him not guilty.

Answer: c) The treatment worked for a while. You can have half a point for **b)** because Pinel tried this too but it wasn't so successful.

In Britain, William Tuke (1732–1822) pioneered better mental-health treatment and in the USA kind-hearted teacher Dorothea Dix (1802–1887) spread the message. A kind-hearted teacher? Yes, they really DO exist! Anyway, by Victorian times there was measly mixed news for anyone who was considered mad...

The good news: The cruel conditions had gone.

The bad news: There were new terrible treatments such as electric shocks, cold baths and senseless surgery (see page 131 for the dreadful details).

The even worse news: You could be locked up for the rest of your life.

Quick queasy quiz

If you were a Victorian woman what could you be sent to a mental hospital for?

a) Refusing to obey your husband.

b) A love of reading.

c) Going for long walks.

105

Awful army hospitals

Mind you, Victorian mental hospitals were luxurious compared to the most horrible hospitals of all time! I'm talking about army hospitals. In times of war, medical supplies were in short supply and any hospital could become a place of horror. Would you fancy being a French soldier in Germany in 1813 during the Napoleonic Wars?

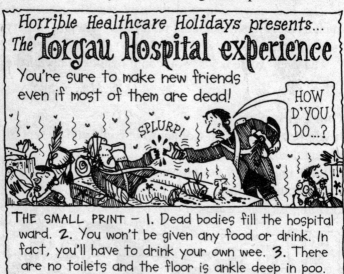

During the Crimean War in Russia (1854) conditions were just as grim at the British army hospital in Scutari. The filthy floor was alive with bugs and chopped off limbs were chewed by dogs. But that's when Florence Nightingale arrived with a team of nurses.

Famous Florence and marvellous Mary

Any old book will tell you that modern nursing was founded by Florence Nightingale (1820–1910) But in this book we're also honouring an unsung hospital heroine – Jamaican nurse Mary Seacole (1805–1881). Flo and Mary met only once, but we've brought them together to tell their stories…

My name is Florence Nightingale.
I'm small and neat and determined.

And I'm Mary Seacole.
I'm big and colourful and determined.

My papa wouldn't let me be a nurse.

I've been nursing all my life - like my mum before me. I started practising on my dolls and cats and dogs.

I pestered Papa until he got me a job in charge of a nice ladies' hospital.

No one got me a job. The army let me nurse its soldiers because my herbal remedies saved their lives.

108

Well-wishers sent me money and supplies.	Nobody sent me anything.
I saved hundreds of lives.	I saved hundreds of lives with my herbal remedies for the deadly diarrhoea diseases - dysentery and cholera.
The wounded soldiers loved me and kissed my shadow.	The wounded soldiers loved me and called me "Mother".
I had to put up with stupid bullying doctors.	I had to dodge cannonballs to rescue wounded men. When I dived for cover I couldn't get up again.
After the war I was hailed as a heroine.	After the war I faced prison because I couldn't pay my bills.

I had it tough...

But I had it tougher!

Any old book will tell you what happened to famous Florence…

After the war she fell ill and went to bed for 40 years. But nothing stopped no-nonsense Nightingale. She raised cash for a nurses' school and wrote a bestselling book telling them what to do. Flo was very good at telling people what to do…

Now even the most dim-witted doctor knows these facts – but do they know the truth about this wonderful woman?

Grrr! Any idiot can do this quiz!

Don't ask me I'm a numbskull...

Flo's true or false quiz
True or false?
1 Florence Nightingale invented the idea of training nurses.
2 She wore her fingers to the bone scrubbing hospital floors.

1 and 2: THIS IS EASY!

3 The number of deaths at the hospital fell, thanks to Florence.
4 She always carried a lamp – that's why she's known as "the Lady with the Lamp".
5 She always carried a hamster in her pocket.

3, 4, 5: Er...

Answers:

ALL the answers are FALSE!

1 Flo wasn't the first to train nurses. For example, Theodor Fliedner and his wife trained nurses in Germany in the 1830s. On the Russian side, devoted doc Nikolai Ivanovitch Pirogoff (1810–1881) also trained nurses.

2 Flo didn't do the dirty work – she was an administrator. Flo's sister claimed she wasn't even a good nurse – but that's sisters for you.

3 The number of deaths actually rose! The hospital had dodgy sewers where germs could multiply, but Flo didn't clean them out. At the time she didn't believe germs caused disease.

4 Flo didn't carry a lamp – she had a crinkly Turkish army *lantern*.

SPOT THE DIFFERENCE

Lantern

AND SPOT THE SIMILARITY...

Lamp

...THEY'RE BOTH... YOUCH... **HOT!**

5 Hamster – pah! No, she kept her pet *owl* in her pocket. She later owned 60 pet cats and I bet she spent a fortune on kitty-litter.

But what about Mary?

Mary was last seen facing jail and I bet you think she suffered a measly fate. But – HOWLS OF AMAZEMENT – here's a Horrible Science story that ends happily! When news of Mary's plight spread, people took her to their hearts. Thousands flocked to a benefit concert. And nothing stopped Mary for long. She wrote her life story and it was bestseller. Thanks to her brilliant book Mary lived happily ever after. Today she's not too well-known but she should be just as famous as famous Flo. In her own way she was even *more* amazing.

Horrible hospitals clean up their act

Thanks to Flo, Victorian hospitals were cleaner than the horrible hospital on page 101. But several pesky problems remained…

Victorian docs and nurses were keen on "bed-rest". This meant you had to stay in bed for weeks on end. Er – hold on I've just been sssh'ed!

Modern doctors aren't so keen on bed-rest. The lack of exercise weakens your bones and muscles, and you get vile bed sores. Personally I think sick children should be made to run errands — the fresh air is good for them you know!

I prefer to be bone idle.

Bet you never knew!

In the 1900s TB patients were sent to special hospitals in the mountains where they had to lie in the sunshine all day. The mountain air was said to be healthy but I bet the patients felt a bit peaky.

Talking about deadly diseases, there's a whole host of them squirming in the next chapter. And I don't think they like us…

WE'RE GONNA GET YOU…

IT'LL BE…

EASY PEASY KILLER DISEASEY!

˙ GRŮESOMĚ GĚRM-BŮSTĚRS ˙

This chapter begins at a very grim time for humans and a very marvellous time for microbes.

Let's take a putrid peek at the past to check out the problems...

A sickly Victorian street

1 Overcrowded slummy houses where you could catch TB by being coughed over.
2 Dirty drinking water full of killer cholera germs.

And conditions were just as measly for the dead. The graveyards were full of deadly disease victims covered only by thin layer of earth. No wonder microbes were having the time of their slimy little lives.

Sickly people poured into big city hospitals. But these were the bad old days and hospitals weren't places you went to get better – they were places you went to get even sicker. Patients perished from infections, and to make matters worse, measly medics didn't understand infection. You could sum up everything doctors knew on the back of a stamp – and here it is.

But at this grim time, in one of these grim hospitals, a dedicated doctor was about to make a dramatic discovery.

115

It would destroy him. His name was Ignaz Semmelweiss (1818–1865), and here's a peek at his secret diary. Oh all right, it might be a forgery…

The secret diary of Ignaz Semmelweiss

1846

I'm working as a junior doctor in the General Hospital in Vienna. I've always wanted to be a doctor and things ought to be wonderful – but they're not. Death is stalking the maternity wards. An awful number of women are going there to give birth … and dying of puerperal fever. Their bodies turn blotchy and fevered and full of pus. What's killing my patients?

A few months later…
One ward is worse than all the others. It's the ward the medical students work in. Women cry and beg not to be sent there. One in three of them will die. The students cut up bodies and then go to the ward to help with births. My fellow doctors reckon bad food or bad air or flowers cause the disease – but I think that's blooming ridiculous. Why should one ward be more dangerous than the other? I think the students are carrying the disease on their dirty hands. But how and why?

GRUBBY STUDENT

1847

My dear friend Jakob Kolletscka is dead. He was dissecting a body when he cut his finger. He fell sick with a disease – it looked like puerperal fever. I think Jakob caught the disease from the corpse when he cut his finger. Now I'm making the students wash their hands.

OUCH! Every day I stand in the doorway of the ward with a bowl of chloride of lime and I won't let them through until they wash their grubby hands in the mixture. It stings their skin but I'm sure it will get rid of the disease. The students don't like it.

"I'm only trying to save lives," I plead. But they won't listen. They only wash their hands because I force them to.

1848

Success! Fewer women are dying of the fever. Washing the students' hands has stopped the disease from spreading. But my boss, Professor Klein, doesn't agree – I'm sure he's only jealous of my success but he's in charge and I can't argue with him. What can I do? I'd be pulling out my hair but I haven't got any!

There was nothing sad Semmelweiss could do and in 1849 he was forced to leave the hospital. The sloppy students went back to their measly messy habits and more woeful women died of the fatal fever.

Semmelweiss got a hospital job in Hungary. Once again he saved lives by making the other doctors wash their hands. But he was starting to act strangely. He wrote a book on his ideas that was full of repetitions and insults. Other doctors thought that Semmelweiss was as mad as his ideas.

In 1865 Semmelweiss was locked up in a mental hospital. No one knows what happened next. Some say he cut his finger during his final operation. Others say he was beaten up or tied up at the mental hospital. All that's certain is that Semmelweiss picked up an infection and died two weeks later. He had been killed by the killer germs that he had fought so hard against.

Fourteen years later in Paris…
A doctor was speaking at a medical meeting. Scornfully the doctor attacked the ideas of Semmelweiss and set out his own explanation for puerperal fever. But then the story goes, a scientist stood up and told the doctor he was wrong…

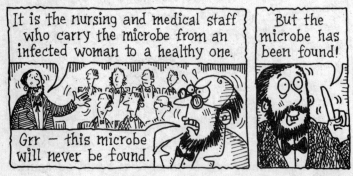

The scientist's name was Louis Pasteur (1822–1895) and he felt sure he had spotted the germ through his microscope. Today we know that Semmelweiss had been right. The measly medics with mucky hands are long forgotten, but every doctor in the world knows the name of Ignaz Semmelweiss.

Mind you, even before Pasteur's work on germs (even before Semmelweiss died although he didn't know it), the evidence that germs cause disease had been piling up. We put a microbe on trial for murder...

A trying time

You are accused of causing deadly diseases...

Not guilty!

Roman writer Marcus Varro (116–27 BC) wrote that marshes were unhealthy because tiny invisible creatures got into the body and caused disease.

He was just guessing!

Italian doctor Girolamo Fracastoro (1478–1553) thought tiny "seeds" that could be spread by contact or blown on the wind caused disease.

I bet he never seed them!

But in 1683 Dutch scientist Anton van Leeuwenhoek (1632–1723) saw microbes through his microscope.

He was being small-minded!

119

French scientist Pierre Bretonneau (1778–1862) thought that each germ caused a particular disease.

 Yeah, right – prove it!

US doctor Oliver Wendell Holmes (1809–1894) claimed that puerperal fever was spread on dirty hands even before Semmelweiss suggested it. But doctors scoffed at his views...

 I'm a bit peckish myself...

Scientist Agostino Bassi (1773–1856) spent 25 years studying caterpillars. He proved that a fungus caused silkworm caterpillar disease and reckoned germs caused other diseases. Doctors didn't believe him.

What a mouldy idea!

Louis Pasteur proved that microbes make beer and wine and milk go off...

 It's time I went off...

And in 1876 German doctor Robert Koch (1843–1910) proved that anthrax bacteria cause the deadly disease anthrax.

 It's a fair cop!

By the 1900s medicine was a fully fledged science, and dynamic doctors prowled the world in search of deadly disease microbes. And they had a powerful weapon to prevent diseases.

Measly medicine fact file

NAME: Vaccination

THE BASIC FACTS 1 Remember those nice old Turkish ladies handing round deadly smallpox pus on page 72? Well, vaccination was an improved way of doing much the same thing. It meant giving the patient a weak or dead germ to get their white blood cells to recognize it in the future. And kill it.

2 The first successful vaccinations were developed by Edward Jenner (1749–1823) in 1796. His vaccine for smallpox used pus from the less deadly disease cowpox.

3 Soon vaccination was saving lives – even before doctors knew about germs.

THE MEASLY DETAILS Cowpox actually started off as a disease of horses. It was spread to cows by people.

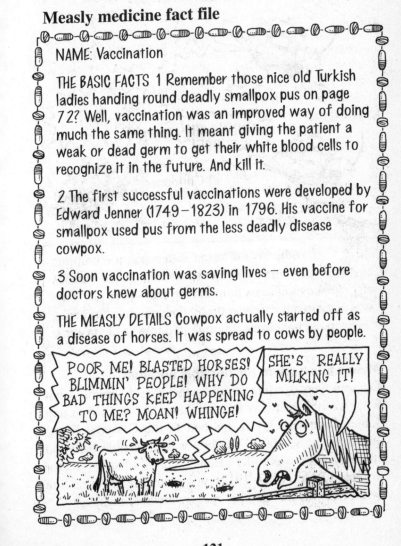

POOR ME! BLASTED HORSES! BLIMMIN' PEOPLE! WHY DO BAD THINGS KEEP HAPPENING TO ME? MOAN! WHINGE!

SHE'S REALLY MILKING IT!

Quick queasy quiz

In 1803 cowpox was taken from Europe to South America to be used as a vaccine. The disease could only be kept alive for the journey if it was allowed to infect living animals. Which animals were used?

a) Cows

MOOOOOO! BLEURGH!

b) Horses

NNNNEIGH! BLEURGH!

I FEEL SICK... BLEURGH!

c) Children

Answer: c) A group of children was given the disease. When the ship reached South America the disease was alive and well – but the children were not so well. The vaccine saved thousands of lives. Oh, and once the children got better they never got smallpox....

Meanwhile back in the horrible hospitals

Doctors were starting to grasp the idea of germs – but what was the best way to wipe them out? In 1865 young James Greenlees lay in his bed in the Glasgow Royal Infirmary in Scotland. The boy was in terrible pain and his only hope was toilet cleaner. That's what his doctor Joseph Lister (1827–1912) was planning to cure him with. But was this another measly medical mistake?

PATIENT NOTES
BY JOSEPH LISTER

Name: James Greenlees

Age: 11

Diagnosis: A hay cart crushed the boy's leg. The bone is badly broken.

Prognosis: Infection is certain ... followed by death. Cutting off the leg might prevent infection. Or it might cause it! Even if he lives, James will be crippled and in pain for the rest of his life.

Planned treatment: I've read about Louis Pasteur's work with microbes. Hmm, I wonder if carbolic acid kills germs? It's great for cleaning out sewers! I'm going to clean the leg with carbolic acid and wrap it in a dressing soaked in the liquid. Then I'll put a splint on the leg to help the broken bone heal. But it's a gamble – will it work?

Six weeks later: James is walking ... on TWO legs. Success! His broken bone is completely healed and he doesn't have to hop. I'm so happy I'm hopping instead. Hopping with joy!

Lister's treatment had passed the acid test – but he didn't stop there. He designed machines to squirt carbolic acid in the air and he tested other germ-killers. But there was a problem. Here's how another surgeon might have seen it.

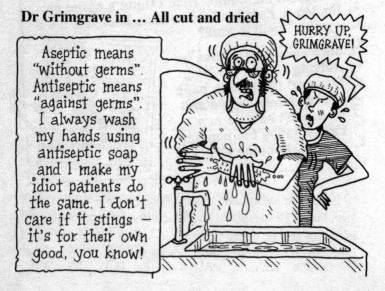

Surgical note 1870

Blast that Lister and his cursed carbolic acid! It stings my skin and makes my throat sore. And if it's not good for germs I'm sure it's not good for me! And that stupid spray is just as bad — my glasses steam up and I can't see where I'm cutting!

I B Stingin, Surgeon

In 1889 a rich, clever American surgeon named William Stewart Halsted (1852–1922) began to develop a new kind of surgery. It was called aseptic surgery. The advantage of aseptic surgery is that you don't have to worry about killing germs during the op, because there shouldn't be any around. Dr Grimgrave is preparing to help with this kind of operation…

Dr Grimgrave in … All cut and dried

Before operations, surgeons **always** "scrub up" using an antiseptic solution to kill germs on their skin.

JUST COMPARE THIS TO THE EARLY OP ON PAGE 94!

Surgeons wear facemasks and talk as little as possible to stop germs spreading in their spit.

NO TALKING, DR GRIMGRAVE!

1 Scalpel with disposable blade. It's thrown away after the op. **2** Surgical instruments have been sterilised with super-heated steam to kill germs. **3** Some surgery is now performed with lasers and since they're made from light they don't get germs at all! **4** Endoscope — a flexible viewing tube allows docs to see what they're doing on a TV screen. Well, it beats daytime telly any day!

Germ-free operating theatres were great for really ambitious ops, and soon surgeons were whipping out stomachs and kidneys and lengths of gut. But some surgeons got carried away and took out bits that were quite happy where they were…

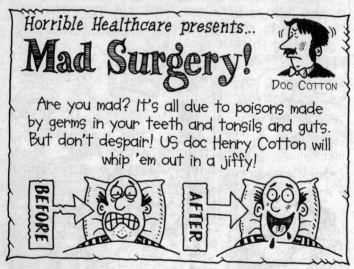

Horrible Healthcare presents...

Mad Surgery!

DOC COTTON

Are you mad? It's all due to poisons made by germs in your teeth and tonsils and guts. But don't despair! US doc Henry Cotton will whip 'em out in a jiffy!

BEFORE

AFTER

In the 1900s Henry Cotton removed healthy body bits from 1,400 people. One-third of them died.

As usual surgeons thought they were doing the right thing even when they were doing the wrong thing. But this wasn't the only measly modern medical mistake. You'll blunder across more of them in the next chapter – make no mistake!

OOOPS!

Have you ever had the sort of up-and-down day in which some things have been great and some things have been a disaster? This kind of measly mixed fortune sums up modern medicine. It's been a marvellous success story, but mistakes are never far away...

Marvellous modern medical milestones

1896 German scientist Wilhelm Roentgen (1845–1923) discovered X-rays.

1916 Pioneer plastic surgeon Harold Gillies (1882–1960) operated on patients. And no, silly, plastic surgeons aren't *made of* plastic. If they were they'd melt!

1930s Chemical germ-killers were pioneered by German scientists. Many of them were based on dye.

1928 Antibiotics were discovered by Alexander Fleming (1881–1955). This was an unhealthy moment for germs and a very healthy moment for the rest of us.

1954 The first kidney transplant takes place. And no, I wasn't talking about the bend in a child's leg – that's a kid's knee.

1961 The first successful hip-replacement ops are done.

1967 The first heart transplant was done by Dr Christiaan Barnard (1922–2001). Now there was man with a heart, well two actually.

1977 The first MRI full body scan takes place (see page 128).

Medical marvel: X-treme X-rays

These high-powered energy rays can travel through flesh but not bone, allowing doctors to take interesting pictures of your skeleton. They're ideal for checking out broken bones or objects such as bullets in the body.

Measly mistake: Rotten rays

X-rays harm the body and too large a dose can kill. But in the 1900s doctors cheerfully used X-rays to blast acne, birthmarks and aching backs. They thought they were healing their patients but thousands were hurt and the rotten rays killed scores of X-ray operators. I guess they became ex-X-ray operators.

X-rays are still in use, although modern machines deliver a smaller dose. And big hospitals have MRI machines (that's Magnetic Resonance Imaging if you're a scientific show-off). These marvellous machines use radio waves and powerful magnets to produce a 3D computer image of your innards. Is that cool or what?

Medical marvel: Super-surgery

In the twentieth century surgery just got better and better…

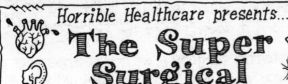

Horrible Healthcare presents...

The Super Surgical Stopover

Come to stay at our super transplant hospital – it's time to make a whole new you!

We've got a new heart, liver, kidney and bone marrow … whatever you want!

Thousands of satisfied customers! In fact everyone's happy except for the donors – and they're usually dead!

SPECIAL GUARANTEE!

If we can't find the organ you want we'll put in an artificial one (this is called an implant).

Lovely choice of artificial hips and other joints – they'll be your flexible friends!

I COULD HARDLY WALK BUT NOW I'M DOING HAND-STANDS!

Granny Grimgrave, aged 93.

Just in – new robot surgeon can do ops. Don't worry – it's controlled by a human surgeon but its hands don't shake and it doesn't need the loo!

SPLURP!

Free plastic surgery – we can reshape your body, give you a new face and even get rid of all that unsightly wobbly fat. You won't recognize yourself!

BEFORE

EH?

AFTER

Measly mistake: Stupid surgery

Does that sound too good to be true? Well, it's not – surgeons can do the most amazing ops. For example… In the 2000s surgeons were giving patients artificial hearts and transplanting voice boxes from dead people to living people.

In 2001 surgeons performed an operation on a man in France. Nothing odd there, except the surgeons were in the US and the actual cutting was undertaken by a remote-controlled robot named Zeus. Well, I guess that robot really proved his metal…

RELAX, GUYS, WHAT COULD POSSIBLY GO WRONG?

VEE COULD AFF A POWER CUT!

But as ever measly medical mishaps do happen…

And even when surgeons didn't botch the op – in the past it was often cruel and unnecessary. Remember those unnecessary ops on page 126? Well, here's a few more…

Brainless brain surgery

Many surgeons believed that they could heal mental illness by surgery. Very often they couldn't.

Some US surgeons cut open the skulls of their patients and zapped their brains with electric shocks. The brains made a snap, crackle and pop as they fried.

US surgeon, James Poppen (1903–1978) tried an op, which was compared to "dipping a vacuum cleaner in a bucket of spaghetti". It was Poppen sucking up bits of fried brain. Anyone for pasta?

DO YOU WANT SOME PARMESAN ON THAT, DOC?

But the most famous brain surgeon of his day was American Walter Freeman (1895–1972). Freeman's op was so revolting I couldn't possibly tell you about it in a respectable educational book like this. What's that? You won't read on unless I do? OK, but don't say I didn't warn you…

MY BRILLIANT BRAIN OP
By Walter Freeman

Important note: The patient doesn't need painkillers - they can even be wide-awake!

1. I pull the eyelid away from the eyeball.

SPLURP!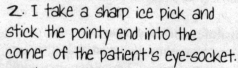

2. I take a sharp ice pick and stick the pointy end into the corner of the patient's eye-socket.

3. Then I push the point to the back of the eye socket.

4. Next I take a hammer ... and bang the pointy end through the bone and into the brain.

5. I waggle the ice pick to and fro to cut the brain from the inside.

6. I tell the patient to wear sunglasses.

☠ HORRIBLE HEALTH WARNING!

Don't even think of practising this operation on small brothers and sisters, or any other helpless furry creature ... It's a really brainless thing to do! If you ignore this warning you will find a new life opening up before you — that's life in prison!

The op seemed to work. The patients had no more mental illness – but then they had no more personality or feelings either. At first Freeman was hailed as a star surgeon but then doctors began to criticize him. In 1967 he used his ice pick on a woman patient for the third time. She died and the dangerous doctor was banned from operating.

Bet you never knew!
In the ten years up to 1955, in the USA alone 40,000 people were given brain surgery. Most of them didn't even need it.

Medical marvel: Miracle medicines

The fight against measly microbes went on throughout the twentieth century, and over the years doctors discovered some powerful new weapons.

First there were chemicals that killed germs… One of the most famous was a red dye called prontosil. German scientist Gerhard Domagk (1895–1964) discovered its germ-killing power in 1932 and tested it on mice. But then his little daughter Hildegard fell ill with blood poisoning. She became the first human saved by the new drug. Prontosil worked fine but it had the unfortunate effect of turning patients bright pink.

133

And then came antibiotics… Antibiotics were even more powerful germ-killing drugs. So if you want to be a dynamic doc you really need the full facts on these marvellous medicines.

Measly medicine fact file

Name: Antibiotics

THE BASIC FACTS 1 An antibiotic is a germ-killing substance made by a fungus or bacteria.
2 The first one was penicillin (so how come you know that already?) But many more have been found since.
3 It wasn't until 1940 that scientists were sure that penicillin could cure disease in humans.

THE MEASLY DETAILS Most scientists ignored Alexander Fleming's work and it nearly got forgotten. And that's not the only measly antibiotic mistake…

Measly mistake: Microbes fight back

Trust Dr Grimgrave to have miserable microbe news for us…

Some bacteria can survive antibiotics better than others. When idiot patients stopped taking antibiotics because they felt better, the surviving bacteria could breed and become tough antibiotic-proof germs known as "superbugs". Of course some doctors made things worse by prescribing antibiotics when they weren't needed.

Er, no thanks, Dr Grimgrave. Oh well, it's lucky we've got a worldwide drug industry to invent new antibiotics…

Medical marvel: Powerful pills
Today the drugs industry develops ever-more powerful medicines to beat germs and ease the symptoms of disease. But some new drugs proved to be dangerous…

Measly mistake: Terrible thalidomide
Just imagine that you're US doctor Frances Kelsey. It's 1961 and it's your first job for the Federal Drug Administration. You have to check the safety of a new sleeping pill. It looks OK, but you've heard reports that it might cause nerve damage.

Quick queasy quiz
What do you do?

a) Ban the drug.
b) Ask for more information.
c) Test the drug on yourself.

Answer: b) Frances asked for more details. The drug company wasn't too happy – they'd already made ten million pills and they wanted them in the shops. But careful Kelsey kept asking for more info even when the company contacted her boss and her job was on the line.

In fact thalidomide damaged unborn babies. When the awful effects of the drug became known Frances Kelsey became a national heroine – she had saved thousands of babies from a terrible danger.

Tragic thalidomide
Sadly thalidomide was sold widely outside the US and 8,000 babies were born to mothers who had taken the drug. Many didn't have proper arms and legs. They faced a painful and uncertain future.

Terry was a British thalidomide baby. He had no arms and legs and only one eye. His mother abandoned him and he lived in a special school. But when Terry was nine he was adopted by an elderly couple named Leonard and Hazel Wiles. Although he wasn't rich, Leonard spent his money building gadgets such as a lifting wheelchair seat to make Terry's life easier. Terry said:

"I would describe my life as a never-ending road with its bumps and smoothness. Sometimes I would be travelling smoothly and then suddenly I would hit a bump of sadness in my life... Then I suddenly met two loving parents who ended my journey and who protected me from life's handicaps. My father is a pioneer in his way because he invents machines to help me and other physically handicapped children to live a normal life."

By the age of 17 Terry could study at college. He could play an electric organ and type stories and do many other things. Other thalidomide children went to university. They played sports and passed driving tests and in time got married and became the parents of healthy children. The story of modern medicine is full of marvels, but the greatest marvel of all is the power of human beings to help themselves.

So now the measly story of medicine has reached the present. But what about the future? Is it looking healthy – or do we need to stock up on sick bags?

EPILOGUE: A HEALTHY FUTURE?

We've been feeding all today's healthcare trends into our supercharged Horrible Science computer and here's what it came up with…

> **HEALTHCARE FORECAST FOR THE NEXT 100 YEARS**
>
> · The war against microbes will go on for ever. We'll never get rid of them and they'll never get rid of us.
> · Thanks to medicine, people will live longer but they may suffer more from diseases of old age.
> · Doctors will carry on trying to develop new treatments. One with a big future could be gene therapy.
> · Some doctors will try out new methods of healing that aren't part of normal medicine.

So what does all this add up to?

1 The war against microbes…

It looks like microbes are here to stay, but that doesn't mean humans can't chalk up the odd victory. In 1980 delighted doctors hailed the final victory over smallpox. A global vaccination push had wiped it off the face of the Earth.

Today the only smallpox germs left are locked away in secure labs never to emerge … we hope!

138

In the 2000s doctors were taking on another killer – polio. When polio hit New York in 1916 no one knew what caused the disease. It often attacked children. They couldn't move, and some of them couldn't breathe. Panicking parents blamed the disease on…

Poisonous centipedes

Smelly sewage whiffs

Mouldy flour

Sour gooseberries

Utter balderdash!

In fact, the disease was caused by a virus that entered the gut when children put dirty fingers in their mouths.

SO WASH YOUR HANDS!

Victims of the disease faced a grim future. Some were crippled for life. Others had to be placed inside metal containers called iron lungs to breathe. US President Franklin D Roosevelt (1882–1945) spent much of his life in a wheelchair, a victim of polio.

But since 1961 polio can be prevented by a tasty vaccination on a sugar lump. In 1988 the World Health Assembly decided to wipe out polio, and by 2006 teams of dedicated doctors armed with sugar lumps and vaccines were hunting down the last traces of polio in Africa and Asia. Soon the killer disease would be a thing of the past. What a wonderful gift for the world's children!

2 People living longer?

Back in the 1800s many people didn't live beyond 40. But today, in richer countries, more and more people are living beyond 100. It's all due to better food, cleaner water and, of course, better medical care.

3 Gene therapy?

Er… Dr Grimgrave what *is* gene therapy?

Sounds like a gene-ius idea!

4 New methods of healing?

There are many kinds of healing outside traditional medicine. For example…

Homeopathy – this means giving patients tiny doses of a substance in order to heal them. Some people swear by this treatment – but could it be a drop in the ocean?

Aromatherapy – this means using scent to relax a patient and promote healing. Some doctors are bit sniffy about this idea.

US doctor "Patch" Adams is famous for dressing up as a clown to make his patients laugh. He believes that laughter helps people to relax and heal faster. Perhaps humour therapy will be on offer in the hospitals of the future.

Dr Grimgrave in … Future shock!

Could this be a glimpse of the future? Well, only time will tell. And that means I don't know. But if I can't tell what'll happen tomorrow, at least I can tell you about the past. And here's what the story of medicine is all about…

The last word on measly medicine

There's an old saying that "doctors bury their mistakes" – but it's not true! They mostly get someone else to bury the bodies. Or they cut them up…

The story of medicine is full of measly mistakes! But there's a better side to it, too. Medicine began with the urge to save lives and despite all the mayhem and mistakes doctors never gave up trying. Eventually a new science of healing emerged. It changed the world and it's still saving lives today.

Happy horrible healing everyone!

Science with the squishy bits left in!

Ugly Bugs • Blood, Bones and Body Bits
Nasty Nature • Chemical Chaos • Fatal Forces
Sounds Dreadful • Evolve or Die • Vicious Veg
Disgusting Digestion • Bulging Brains
Frightening Light • Shocking Electricity
Deadly Diseases • Microscopic Monsters
Killer Energy • The Body Owner's Handbook
The Terrible Truth About Time
Space, Stars and Slimy Aliens • Painful Poison
The Fearsome Fight For Flight • Angry Animals

Specials
Suffering Scientists
Explosive Experiments
The Awfully Big Quiz Book
Really Rotten Experiments

Two horrible books in one
Ugly Bugs and Nasty Nature
Blood, Bones and Body Bits and Chemical Chaos
Frightening Light and Sounds Dreadful
Bulging Brains and Disgusting Digestion
Microscopic Monsters and Deadly Diseases
Killer Energy and Shocking Electricity

Large-format colour hardback
The Stunning Science of Everything